Collins

11+ Non-Verbal Reasoning

Quick Practice Tests
Ages 10-11
Book 2

Beatrix Woodhead

Contents

About this book 3	Test 13 33
Test 1 4	Test 14 35
Test 2 6	Test 15 38
Test 3 9	Test 16 40
Test 4 11	Test 17 42
Test 5 13	Test 18 44
Test 6 15	Test 19 47
Test 7 17	Test 20 49
Test 8 19	Test 21 51
Test 9 22	Test 22 54
Test 10 24	Test 23 56
Test 11 27	Test 24 59
Test 12 30	Answers 63

ACKNOWLEDGEMENTS

The author and publisher are grateful to the copyright holders for permission to use quoted materials and images.

Every effort has been made to trace copyright holders and obtain their permission for the use of copyright material. The author and publisher will gladly receive information enabling them to rectify any error or omission in subsequent editions. All facts are correct at time of going to press.

Published by Collins
An imprint of HarperCollins*Publishers* Limited
1 London Bridge Street
London SE1 9GF

HarperCollins*Publishers*
Macken House, 39/40 Mayor Street Upper,
Dublin 1, D01 C9W8, Ireland

ISBN: 9780008701215

First published 2025

10 9 8 7 6 5 4 3 2 1

© HarperCollins*Publishers* Limited 2025

British Library Cataloguing in Publication Data.

A CIP record of this book is available from the British Library.

Author: Beatrix Woodhead
Publisher: Clare Souza
Project Manager: Richard Toms
Cover Design: Sarah Duxbury and Kevin Robbins
Layout and Artwork: Ian Wrigley
Production: Bethany Brohm
Printed in India by Multivista Global Pvt. Ltd.

About this book

Familiarisation with 11+ test-style questions is a critical step in preparing your child for the 11+ selection tests. This book gives children lots of opportunities to test themselves in short, manageable bursts, helping to build confidence and improve the chance of test success.

It contains 24 tests designed to develop key non-verbal reasoning skills.

- Each test is designed to be completed within a short amount of time. Frequent, short bursts of revision are found to be more productive than lengthier sessions.

- GL Assessment tests can be quite time-pressured so these practice tests will help your child become accustomed to this style of questioning.

- We recommend your child uses a pencil to complete the tests, so that they can rub out the answers and try again at a later date if necessary.

- Children will need a pencil and a rubber to complete the tests as well as some spare paper for rough working. They will also need to be able to see a clock/watch and should have a quiet place in which to do the tests.

- Answers to every question are provided at the back of the book, with explanations given where appropriate.

- After completing the tests, children should revisit their weaker areas and attempt to improve their scores and timings.

For more information about 11+ preparation and other practice resources available from Collins, go to our website at:

collins.co.uk/11plus

Test 1

You have 5 minutes to complete this test.

You have 10 questions to complete within the given time.

There are two figures on the left with an arrow between them. The second figure is related to the first.

There is then a third figure followed by an arrow and five more figures.

Decide which figure (A, B, C, D or E) is related to the third figure in the same way as the first two figures are related. Circle the letter below it.

EXAMPLE

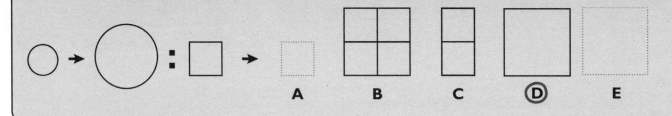

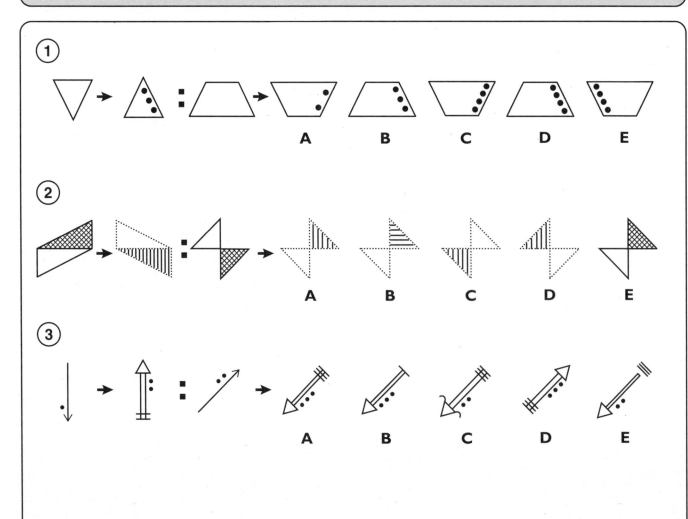

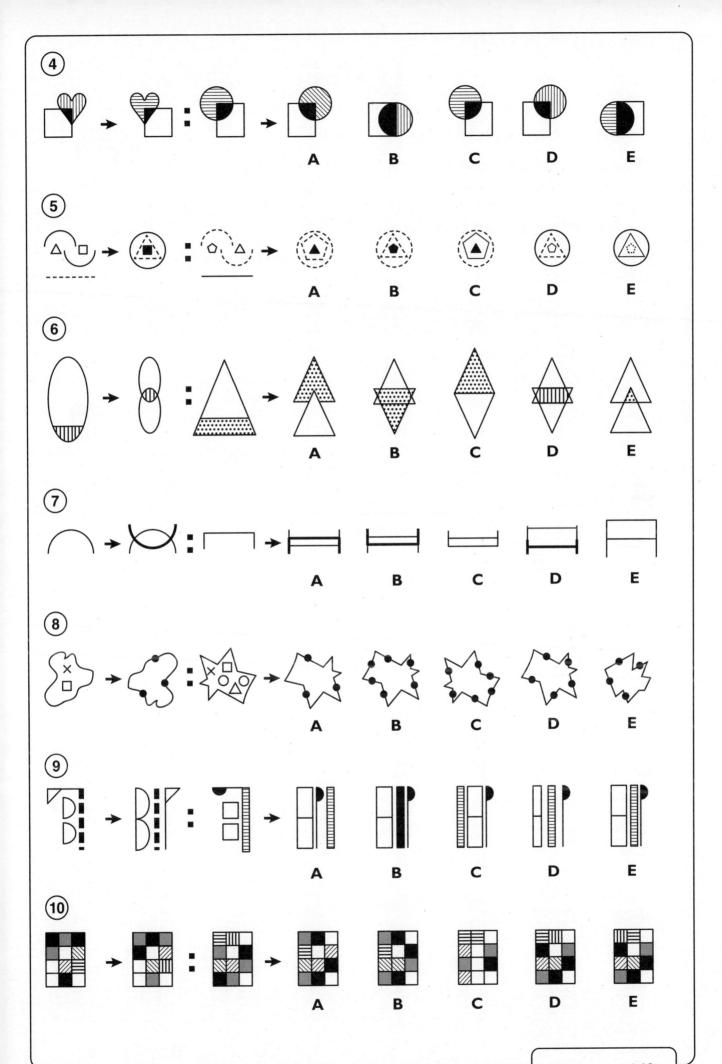

Test 2

You have **6** minutes to complete this test.

You have **12** questions to complete within the given time.

In each grid, one square has been left empty.

Look at the five squares to the right. Decide which one completes the grid and circle the letter below it.

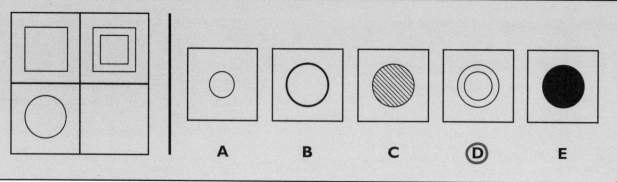

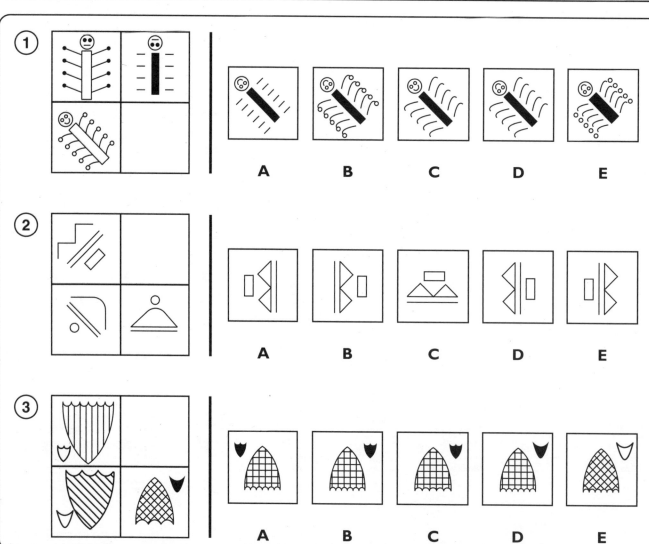

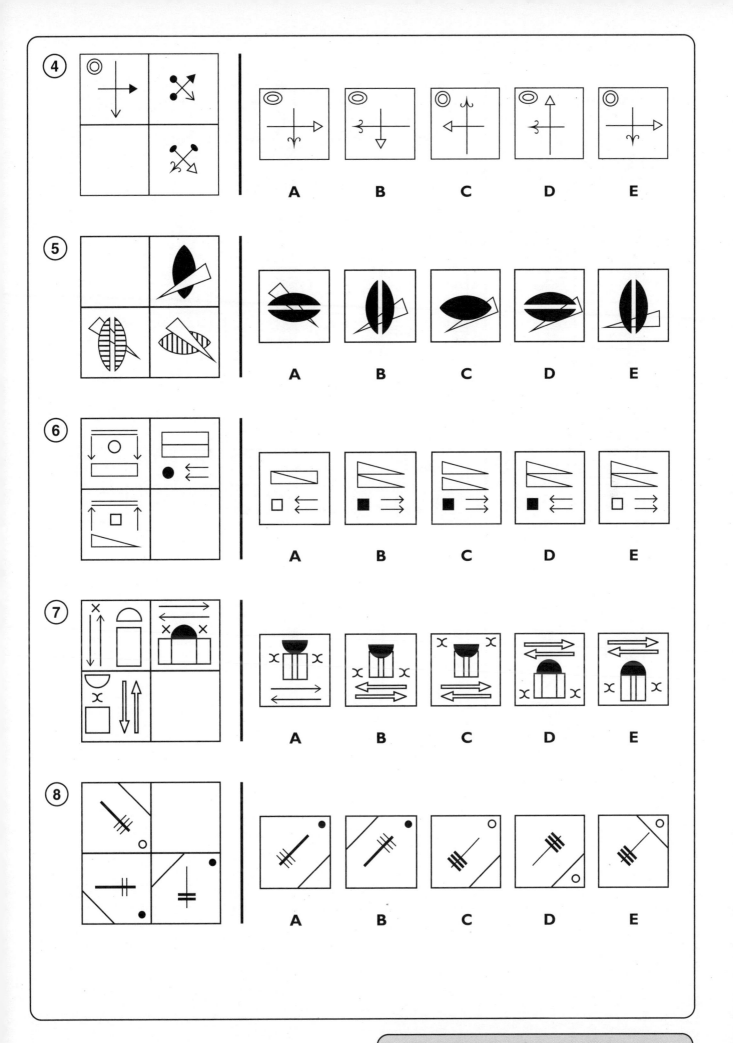

Questions continue on next page

7

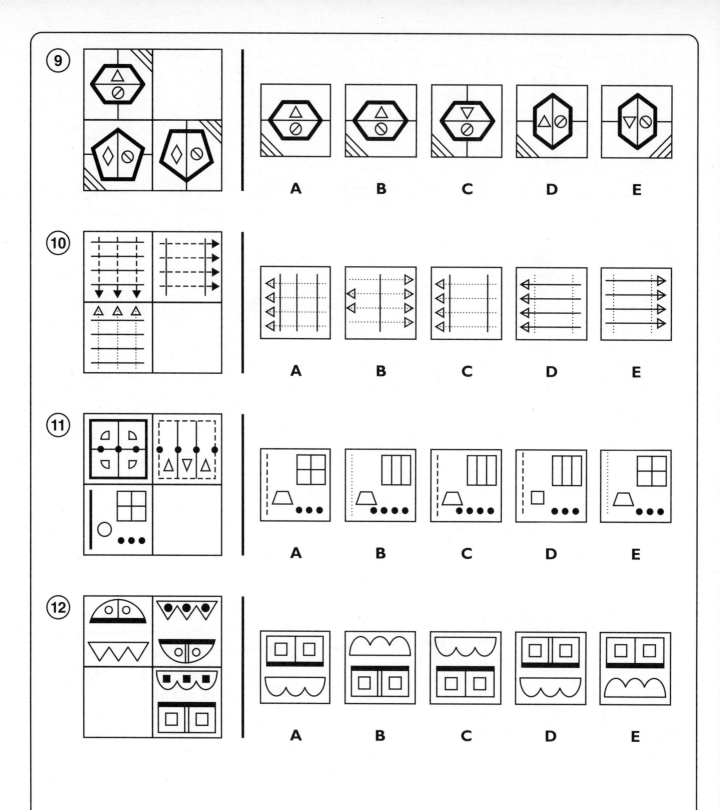

Test 3

You have 5 minutes to complete this test.

You have 10 questions to complete within the given time.

In each question, there is a sequence of squares with one square left empty.

Decide which of the five squares on the right completes the sequence and circle the letter below it.

EXAMPLE

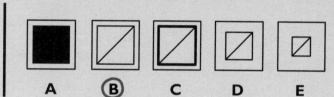

①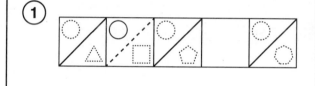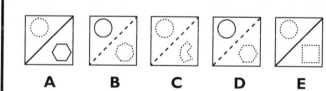

②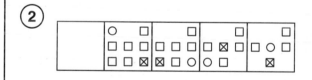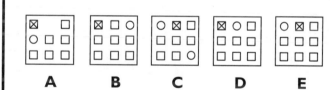

③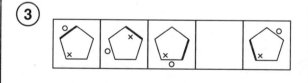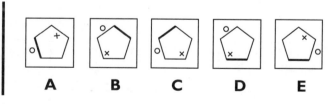

④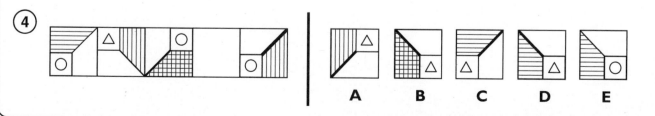

Questions continue on next page

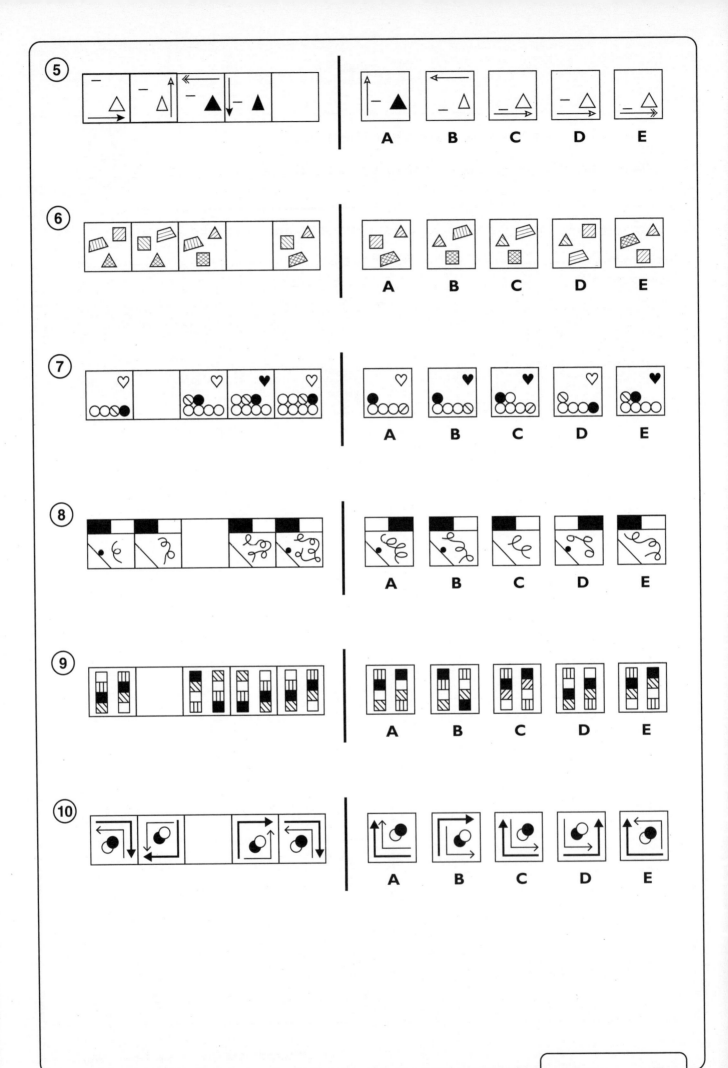

Score: .... / 10

Test 4

You have 5 minutes to complete this test.

You have 10 questions to complete within the given time.

The two figures on the left are similar in some way.

Decide which figure is most similar to the two on the left and circle the letter below it.

EXAMPLE

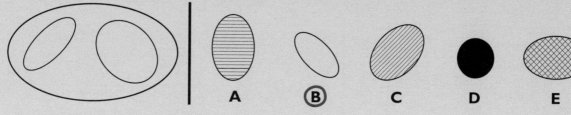

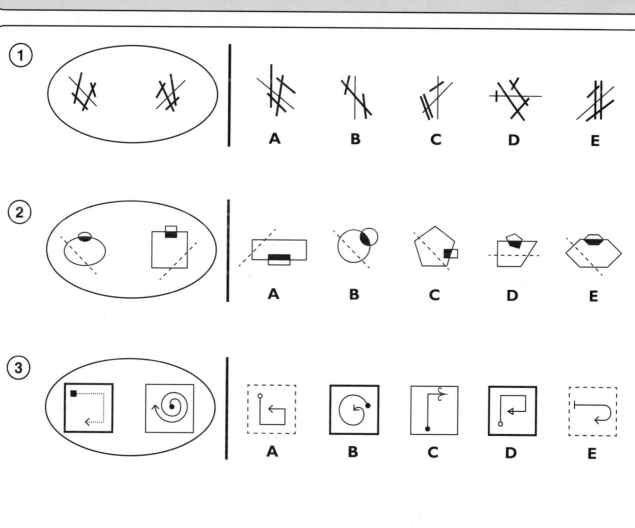

Questions continue on next page

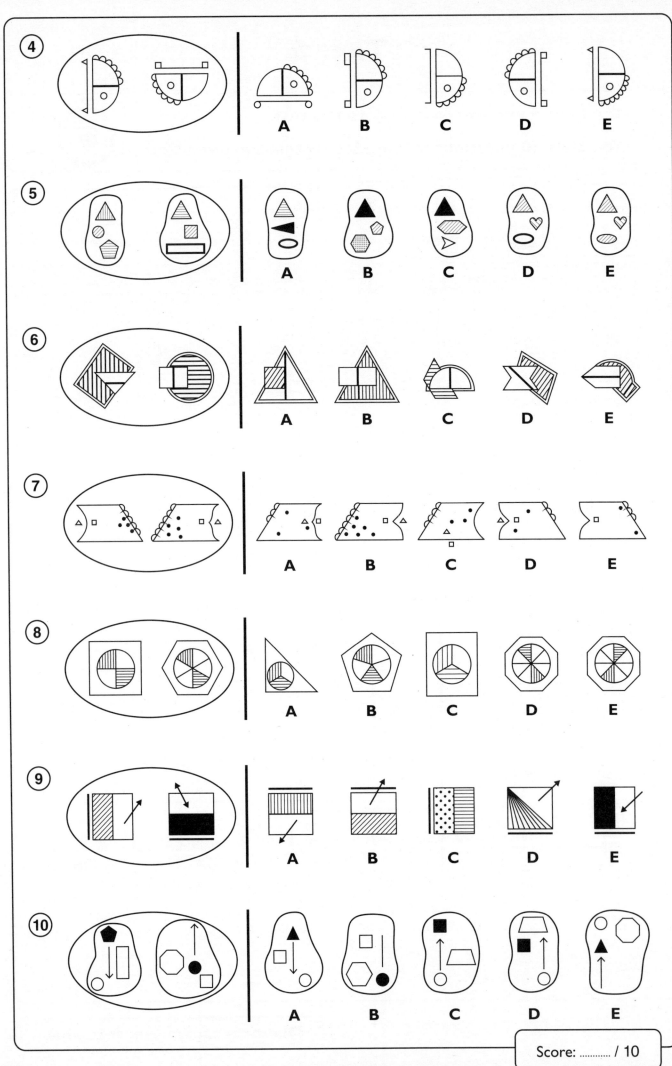

Score: .... / 10

Test 5

You have 5 minutes to complete this test.

You have 10 questions to complete within the given time.

To answer these questions, you have to work out a code.

For the figures on the left, decide how the code letters match the figures. Look at the next figure and work out the missing code. Circle the letter below the correct code.

EXAMPLE

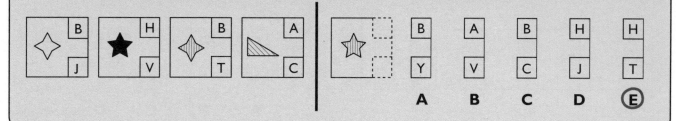

1

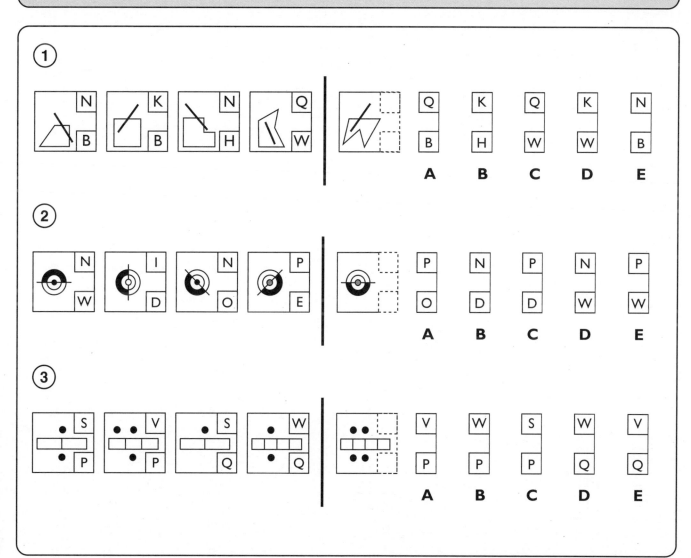

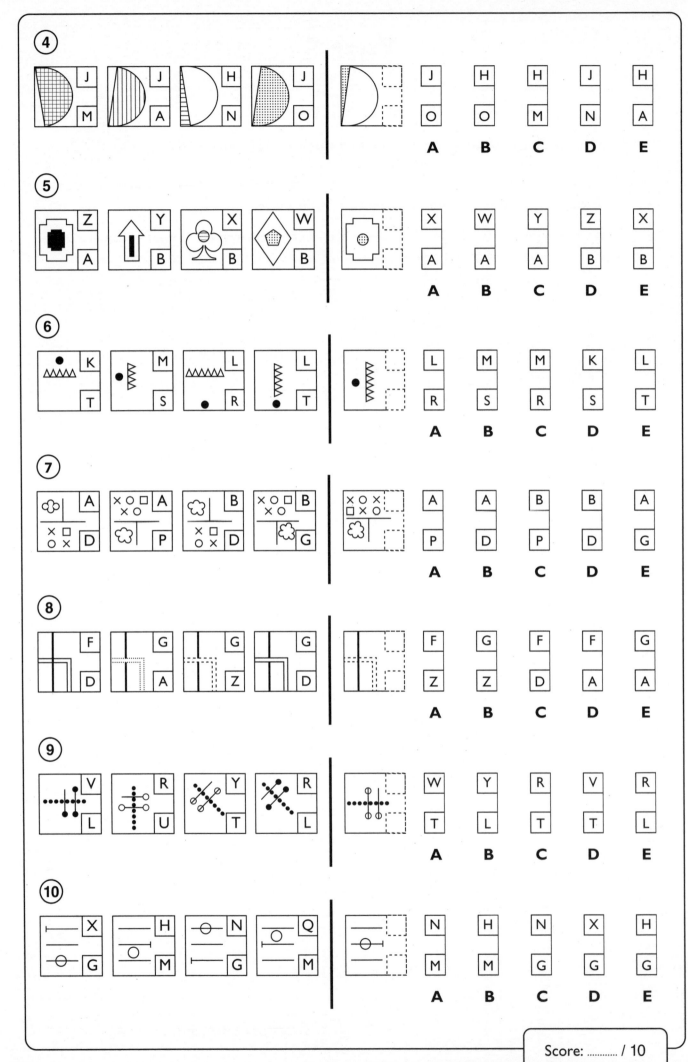

Score: .... / 10

Test 6

You have 5 minutes to complete this test.

You have 10 questions to complete within the given time.

Decide which figure is most unlike the others. Circle the letter below it.

EXAMPLE

A B C D E

①

    A   B   C   D   E

②

    A   B   C   D   E

③

    A   B   C   D   E

④

    A   B   C   D   E

Questions continue on next page

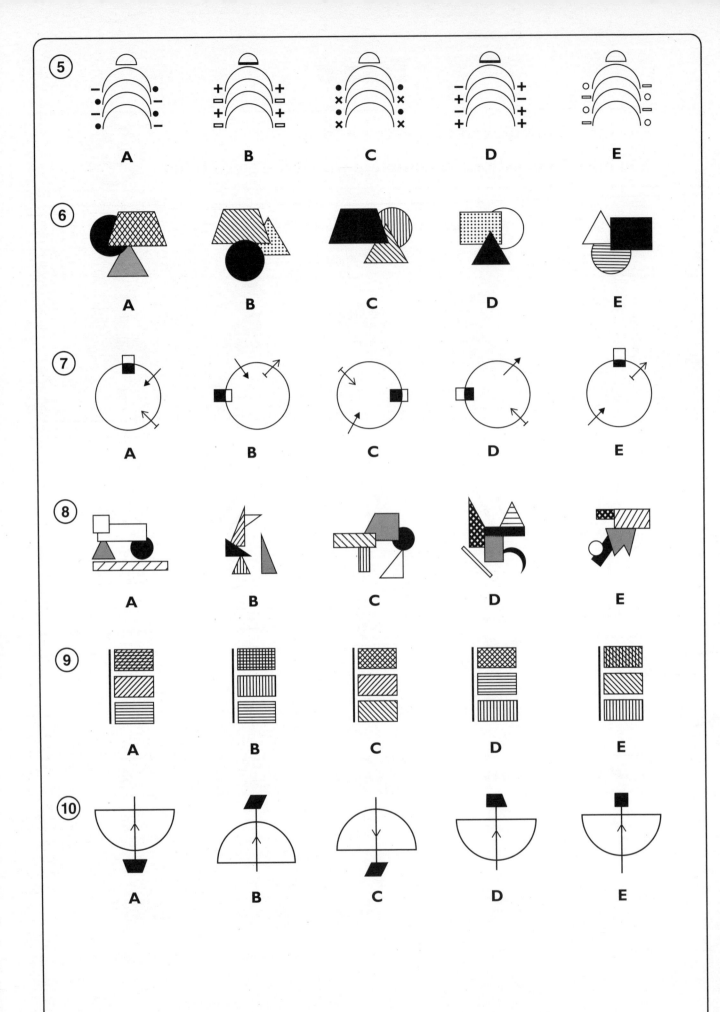

Score: .... / 10

Test 7

You have 5 minutes to complete this test.

You have 10 questions to complete within the given time.

The three figures on the left are similar in some way.

Decide which figure is most similar to the three on the left and circle the letter below it.

EXAMPLE

A B C D E

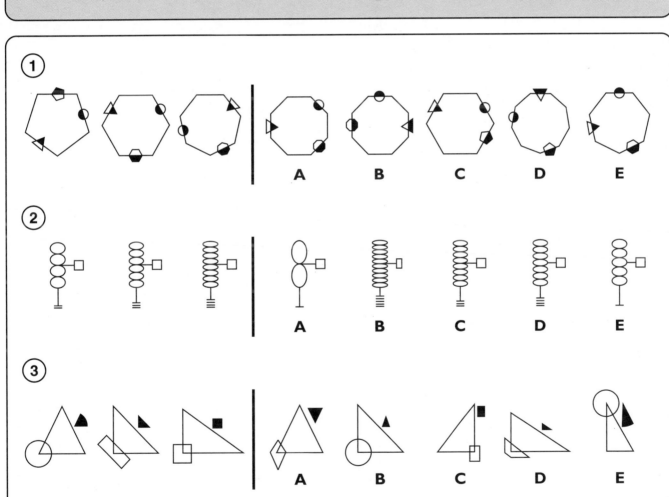

Questions continue on next page

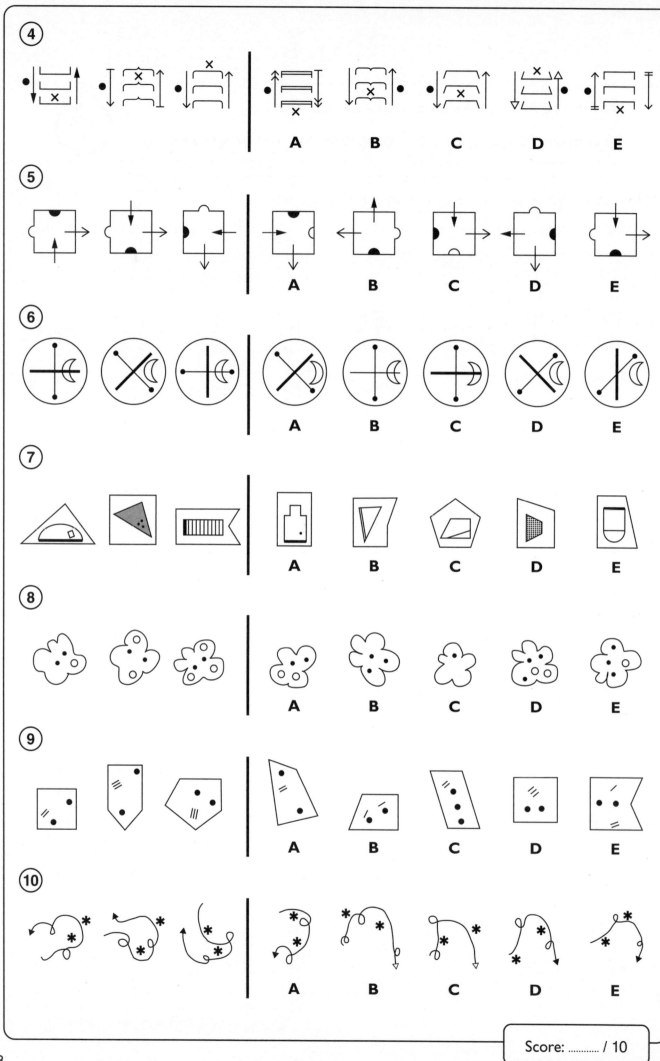

Test 8

You have 5 minutes to complete this test.

You have 10 questions to complete within the given time.

Each figure on the left has a code next to it. Decide how the code letters match the shapes.

Look at the shape on the right and work out its code. Circle the letter below the correct code.

CP

YF

RP

CF	RY	RP	YP	YF
A	B	C	(D)	E

---

①  PXS

YBD

OXD

OXD	YXD	YXS	PXD	OBS
A	B	C	D	E

---

② 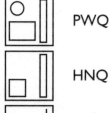 PWQ

HNQ

PNZ

TWQ

PWZ	HWZ	HNZ	PNQ	TWQ
A	B	C	D	E

Questions continue on next page

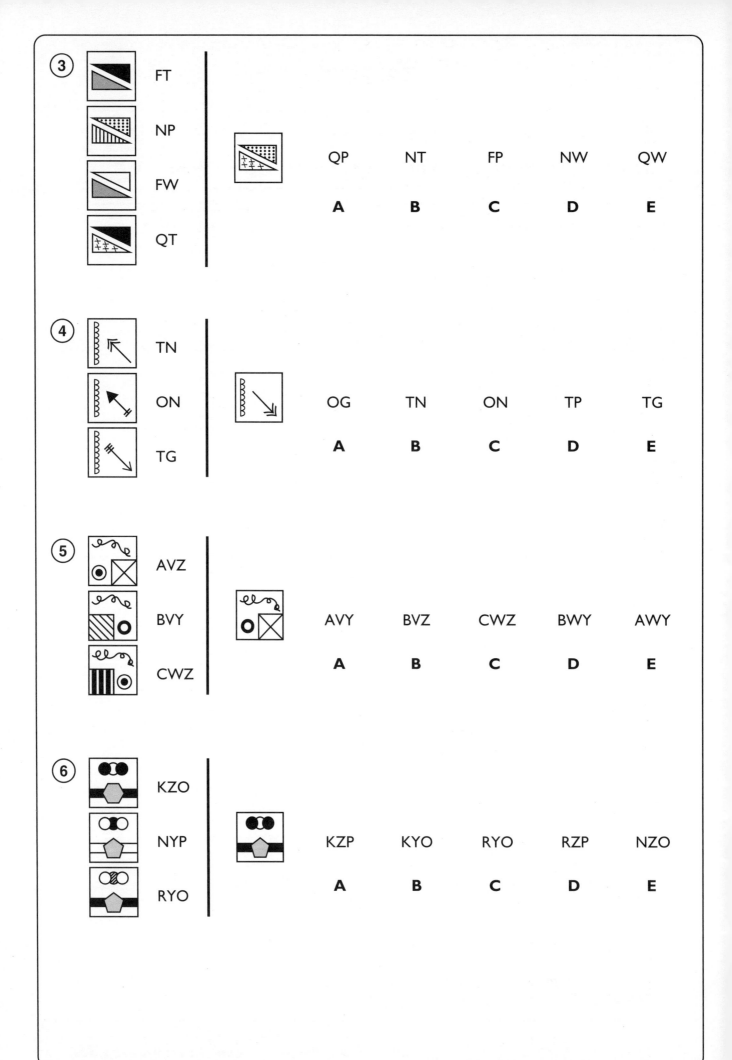

3

FT				
NP				
FW				
QT				

QP	NT	FP	NW	QW
A	**B**	**C**	**D**	**E**

4

TN				
ON				
TG				

OG	TN	ON	TP	TG
A	**B**	**C**	**D**	**E**

5

AVZ				
BVY				
CWZ				

AVY	BVZ	CWZ	BWY	AWY
A	**B**	**C**	**D**	**E**

6

KZO				
NYP				
RYO				

KZP	KYO	RYO	RZP	NZO
A	**B**	**C**	**D**	**E**

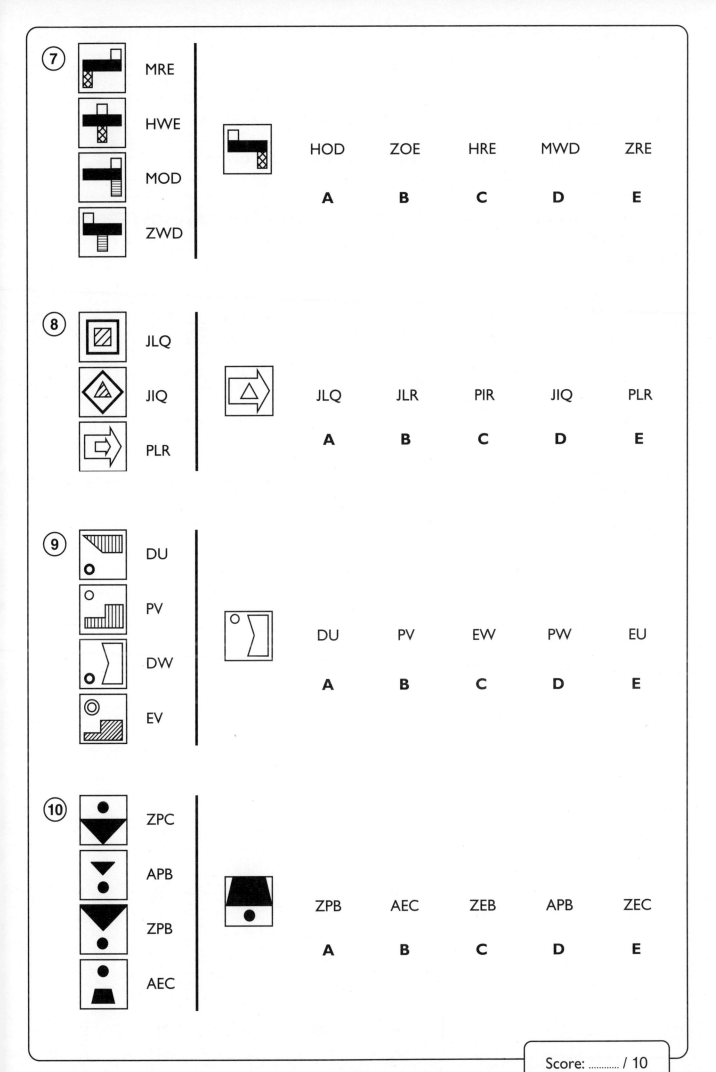

7 MRE / HWE / MOD / ZWD

HOD	ZOE	HRE	MWD	ZRE
A	**B**	**C**	**D**	**E**

8 JLQ / JIQ / PLR

JLQ	JLR	PIR	JIQ	PLR
A	**B**	**C**	**D**	**E**

9 DU / PV / DW / EV

DU	PV	EW	PW	EU
A	**B**	**C**	**D**	**E**

10 ZPC / APB / ZPB / AEC

ZPB	AEC	ZEB	APB	ZEC
A	**B**	**C**	**D**	**E**

Score: .... / 10

21

Test 9

You have **5 minutes** to complete this test.

You have **10 questions** to complete within the given time.

Look at the first figure on the left. Decide how it can be formed by adding one of the answer options to the second figure on the left. The answer options may be rotated but not reflected.

Circle the letter below the correct answer.

EXAMPLE

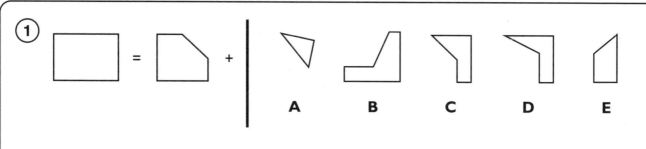

①

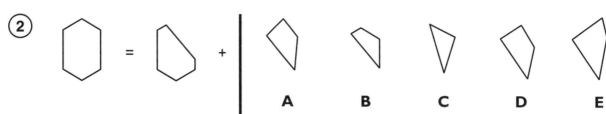

②

③

④

22

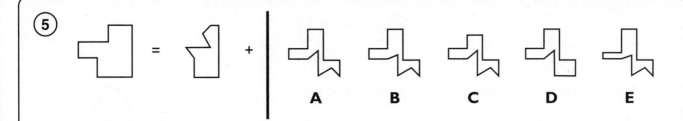

5 ☐ = ☐ + A · B · C · D · E

6 ◇ = ◇ + A · B · C · D · E

7 ▱ = ◇ + A · B · C · D · E

8 ⬠ = ◇ + A · B · C · D · E

9 △ = ⋀ + A · B · C · D · E

10 ⬡ = ⋀ + A · B · C · D · E

Score: .... / 10

Test 10

You have 5 minutes to complete this test.

You have 10 questions to complete within the given time.

Look at the hexagonal grid in each question. Decide which of the hexagons on the right would complete the pattern in the grid.

Circle the letter below the correct answer.

EXAMPLE

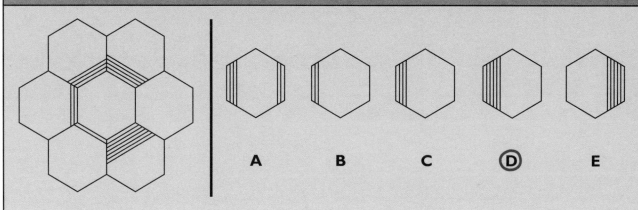

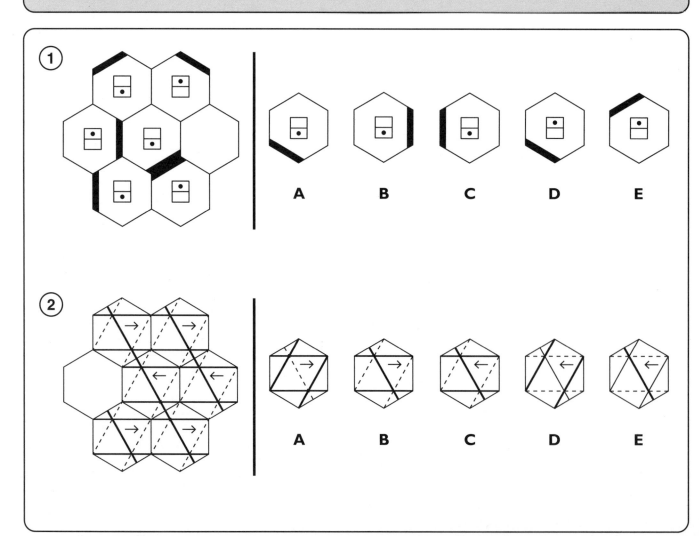

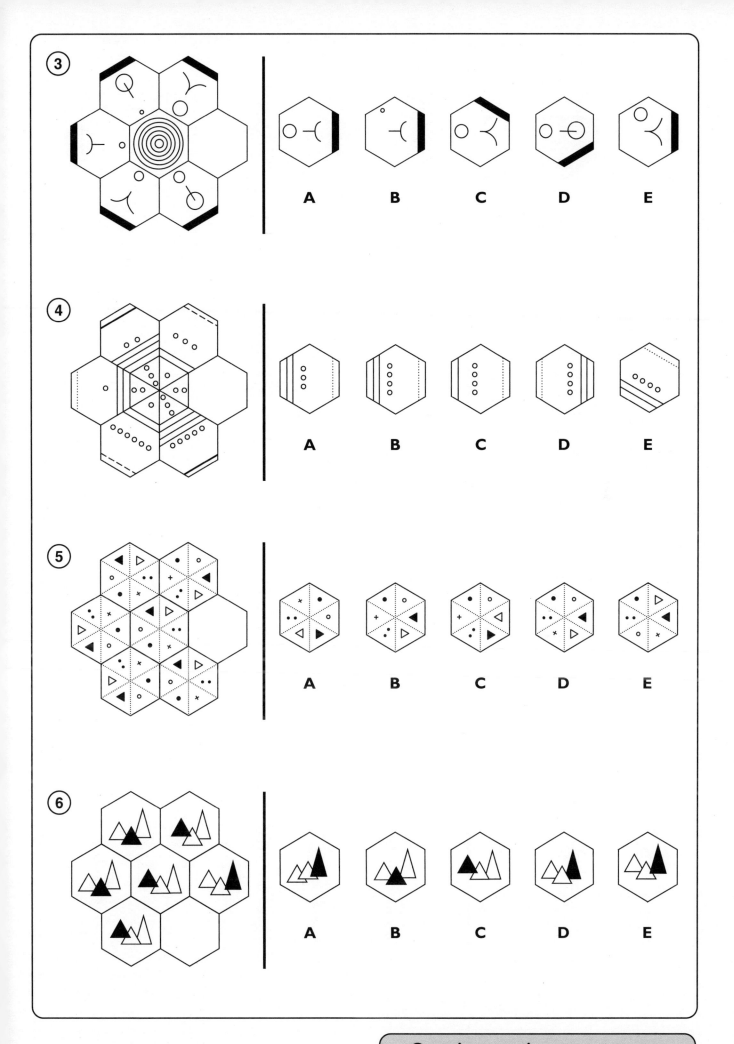

Questions continue on next page

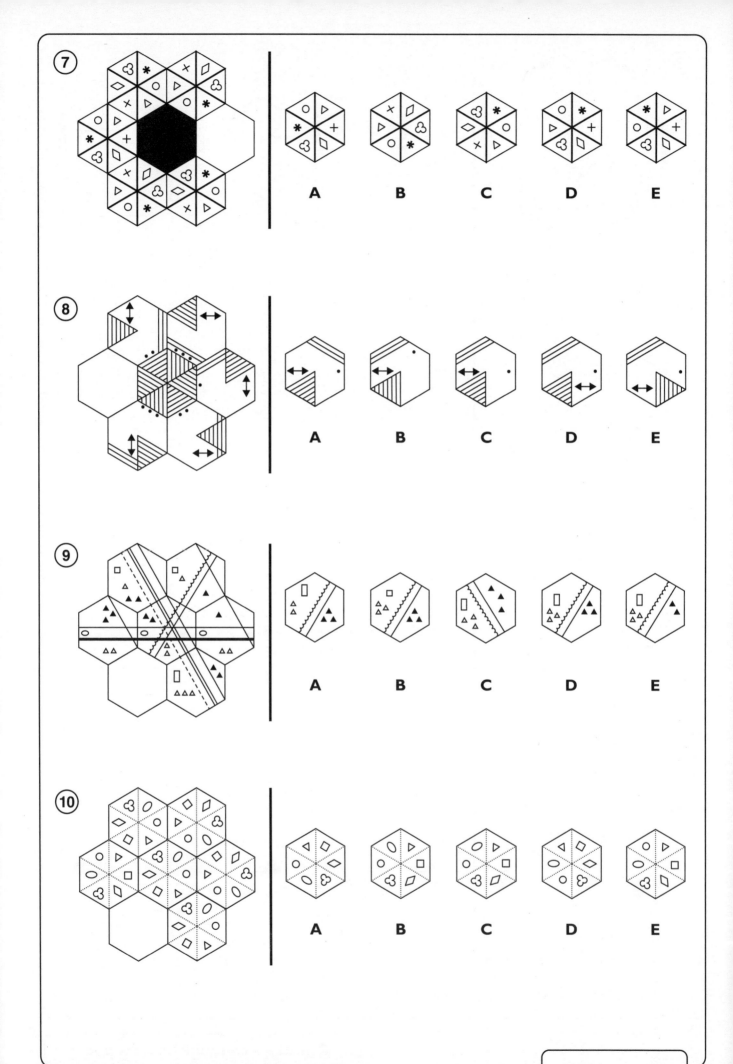

Test 11

You have 6 minutes to complete this test.

You have 12 questions to complete within the given time.

In the star grids, one triangle has been left empty.

Decide which triangle completes the pattern in the grid and circle the letter below it.

EXAMPLE

A   B   C   D   E

(A) is circled.

①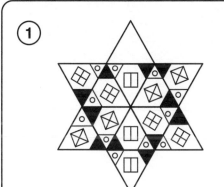

A   B   C   D   E

②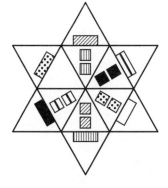

A   B   C   D   E

Questions continue on next page

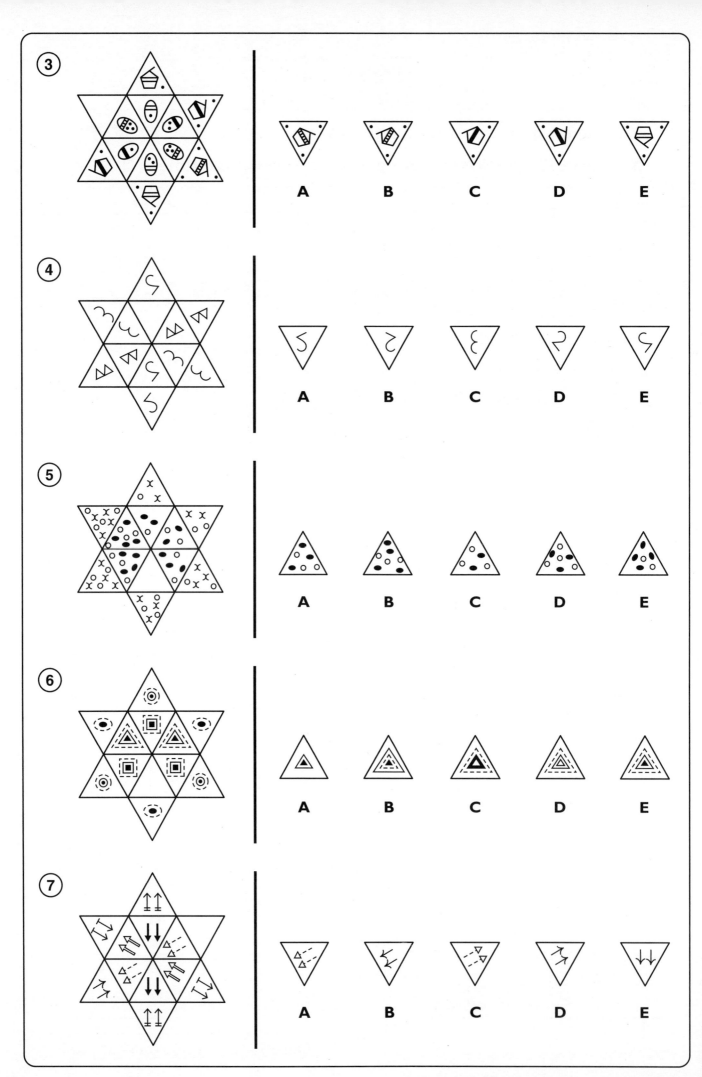

3

A B C D E

4

A B C D E

5

A B C D E

6

A B C D E

7

A B C D E

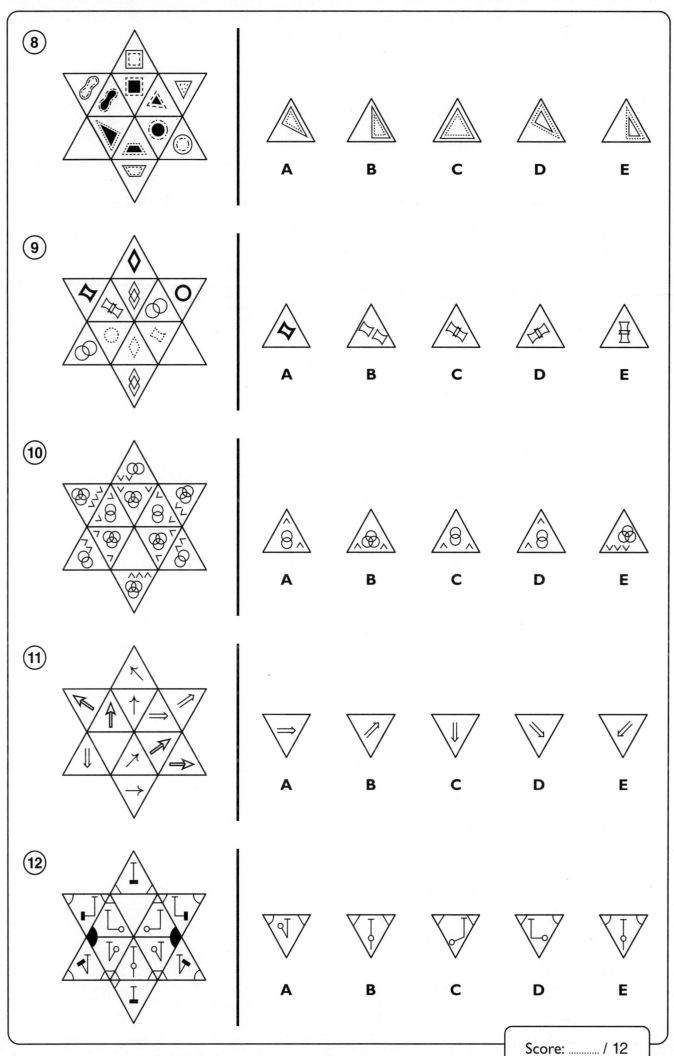

Test 12

You have 6 minutes to complete this test.

You have 12 questions to complete within the given time.

Compare the two large triangles on the left and work out the relationship between them.

Decide which small triangle completes the second large triangle and circle the letter below it.

EXAMPLE

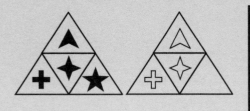

A   B   C   D   E

①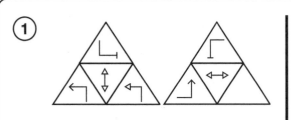

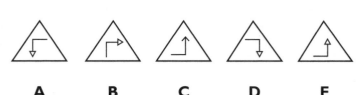

A   B   C   D   E

②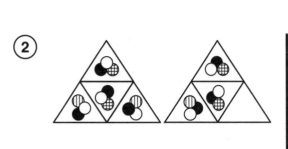

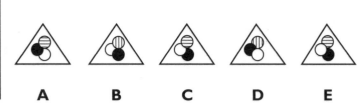

A   B   C   D   E

③

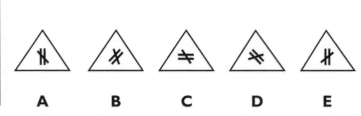

A   B   C   D   E

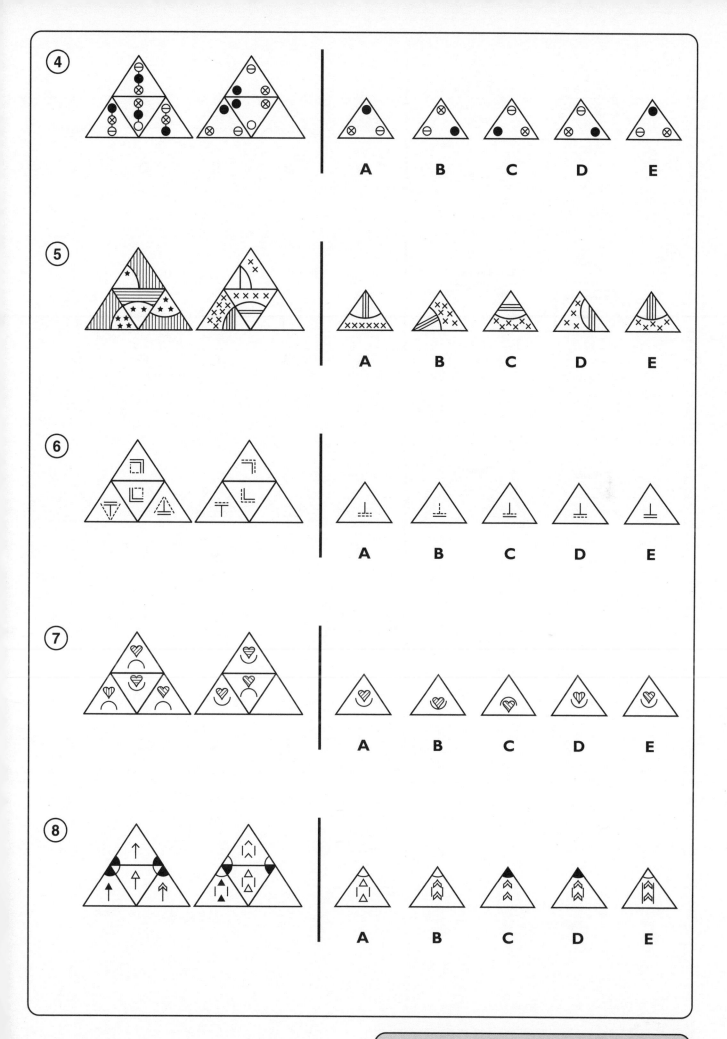

Questions continue on next page

9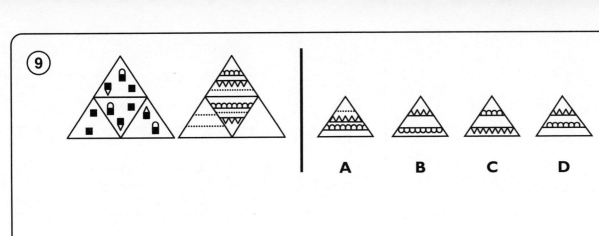

                                  A   **B**   **C**   **D**   **E**

10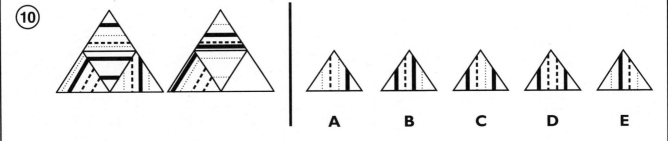

                                  A   **B**   **C**   **D**   **E**

11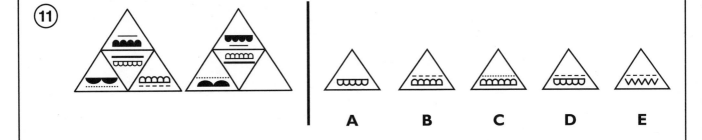

                                  A   **B**   **C**   **D**   **E**

12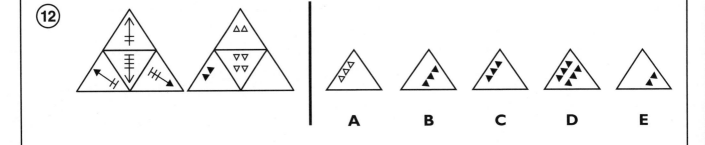

                                  A   **B**   **C**   **D**   **E**

Test 13

You have 5 minutes to complete this test.

You have 10 questions to complete within the given time.

Look at each given net.

Decide which cube can be made from the net and circle the letter below it.

Questions continue on next page

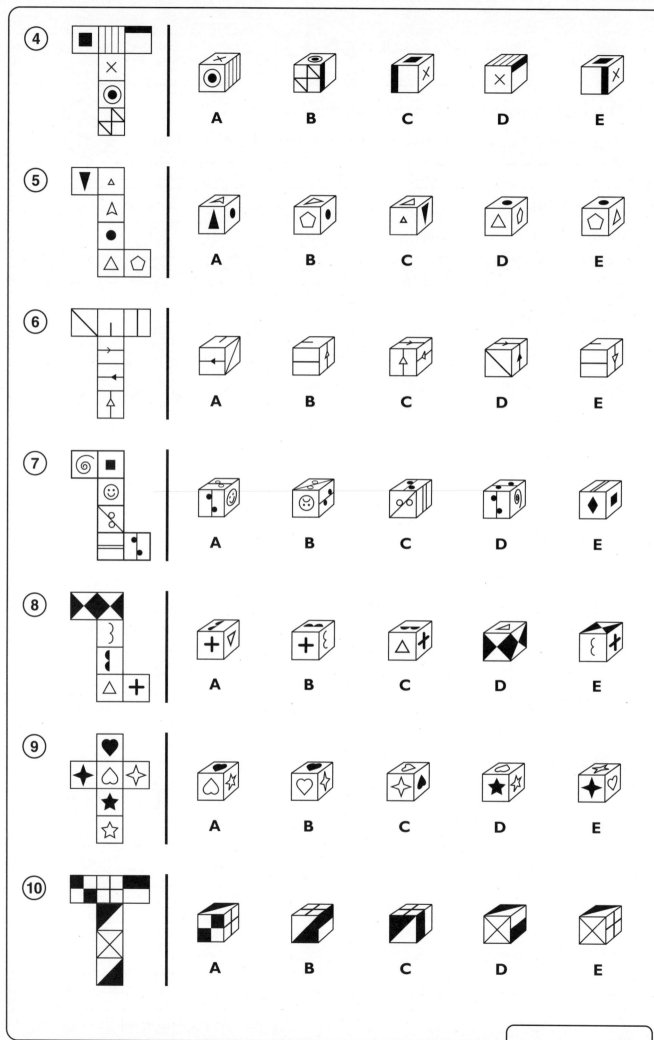

Score: .... / 10

Test 14

You have 5 minutes to complete this test.

You have 10 questions to complete within the given time.

In each diagram, the blocks are all the same size and shape. Some blocks may be hidden from view, supporting blocks above. Decide which answer option correctly shows how many blocks are in the diagram and circle the letter below it.

EXAMPLE

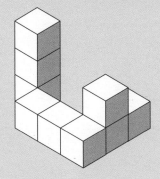

10	13	11	9	12
A	B	C	(D)	E

1

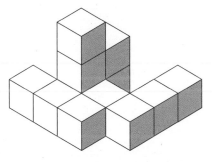

10	12	9	11	13
A	B	C	D	E

2

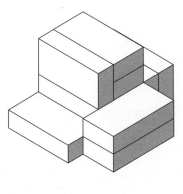

8	12	9	11	10
A	B	C	D	E

Questions continue on next page

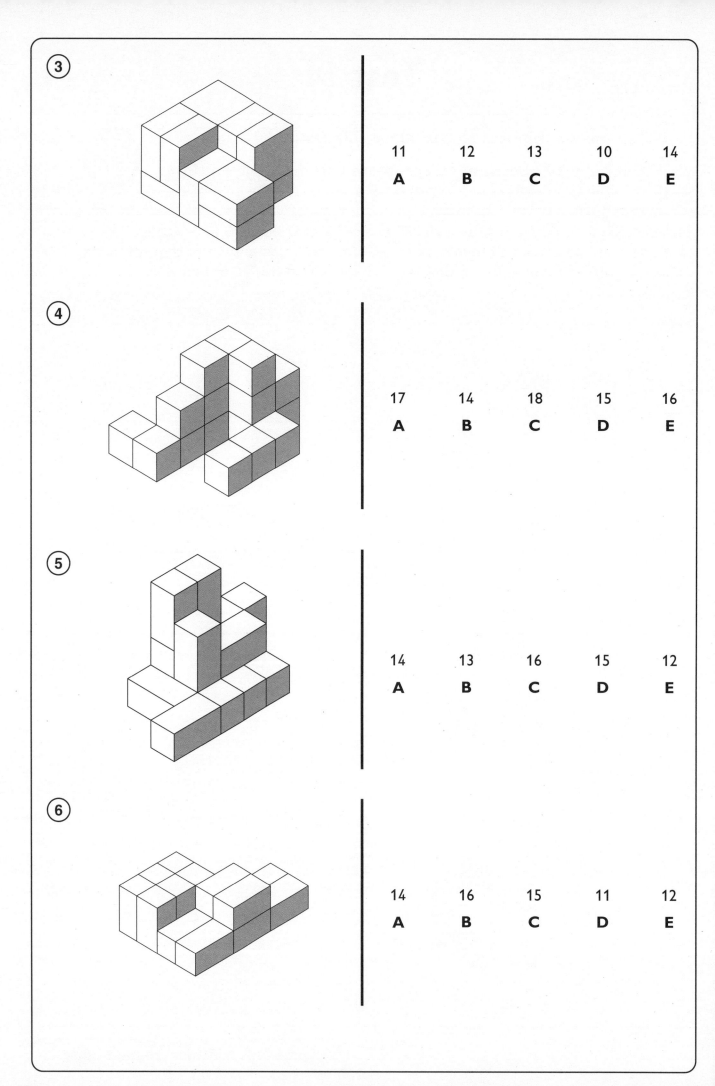

③

11	12	13	10	14
A	**B**	**C**	**D**	**E**

④

17	14	18	15	16
A	**B**	**C**	**D**	**E**

⑤

14	13	16	15	12
A	**B**	**C**	**D**	**E**

⑥

14	16	15	11	12
A	**B**	**C**	**D**	**E**

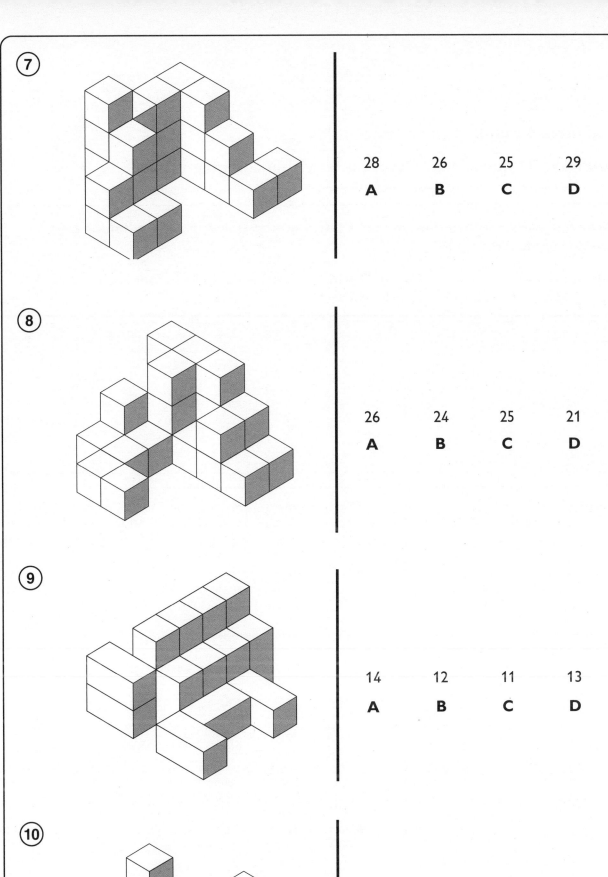

(7)

28	26	25	29	27
A	**B**	**C**	**D**	**E**

(8)

26	24	25	21	22
A	**B**	**C**	**D**	**E**

(9)

14	12	11	13	15
A	**B**	**C**	**D**	**E**

(10)

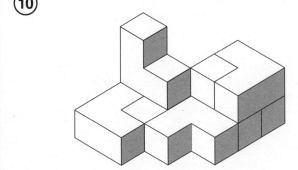

9	8	7	6	10
A	**B**	**C**	**D**	**E**

Score: .... / 10

Test 15

You have **6** minutes to complete this test.

You have **12** questions to complete within the given time.

Look at the square of paper shown on the left. Look at how it has been folded and some holes punched through.

Imagine the paper has been unfolded. Decide which figure on the right shows what it would look like and circle the letter below it.

EXAMPLE

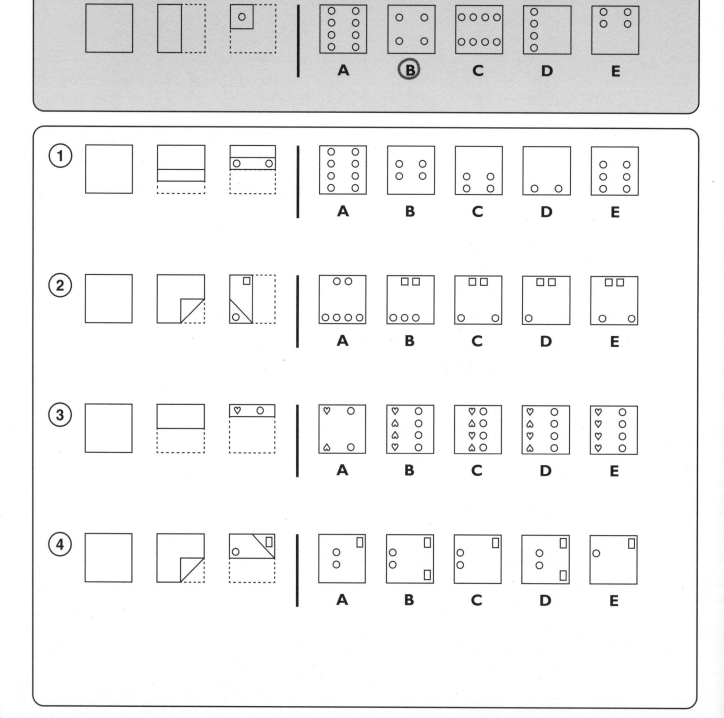

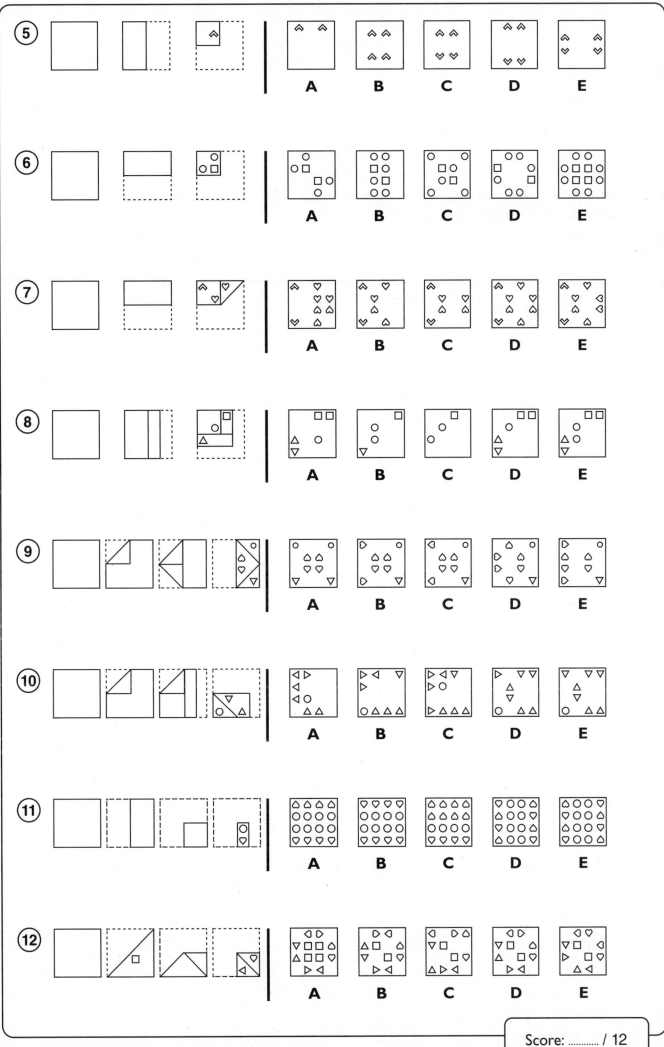

Test 16

You have 5 minutes to complete this test.

You have 10 questions to complete within the given time.

Decide which answer option shows how each 3D figure would appear in a top-down (plan) view. Circle the letter below it.

EXAMPLE

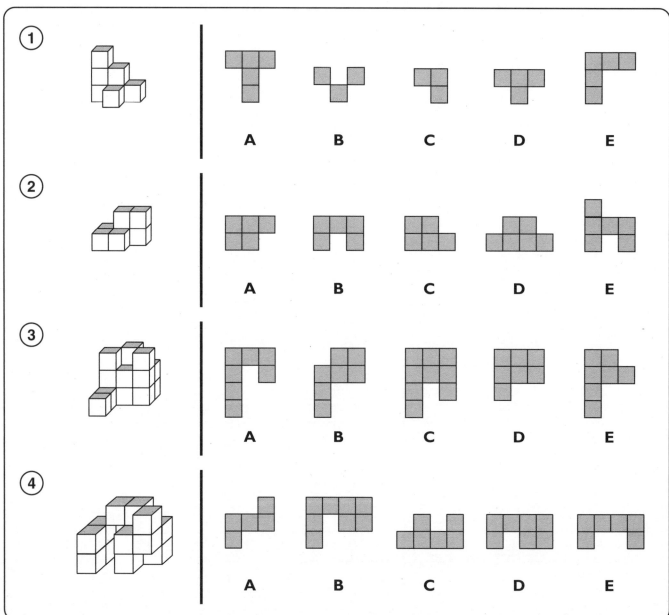

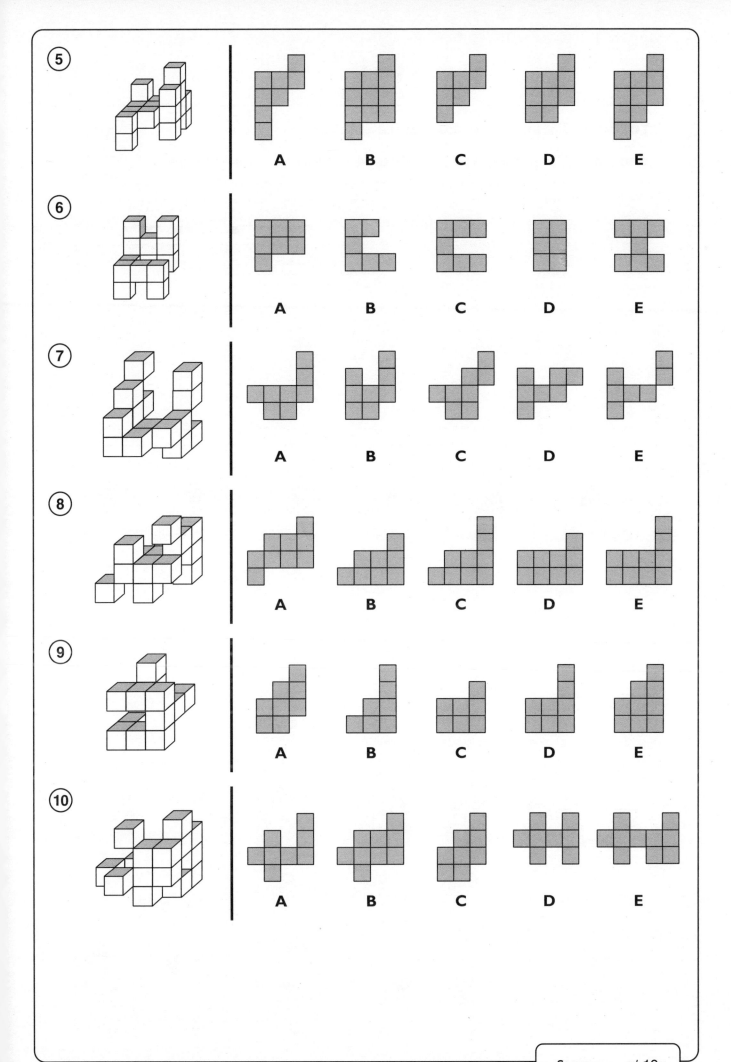

5 A B C D E

6 A B C D E

7 A B C D E

8 A B C D E

9 A B C D E

10 A B C D E

Score: .... / 10

41

Test 17

You have 5 minutes to complete this test.

You have 10 questions to complete within the given time.

Decide which figure is a rotation of the figure on the left and circle the letter below it.

EXAMPLE

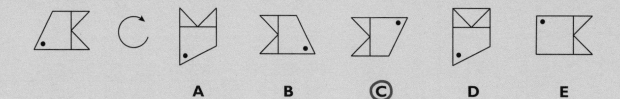

A   B   Ⓒ   D   E

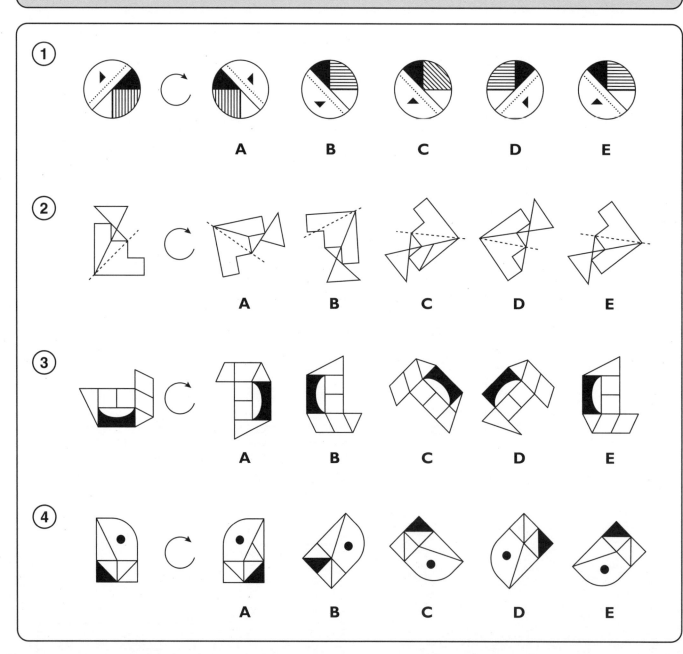

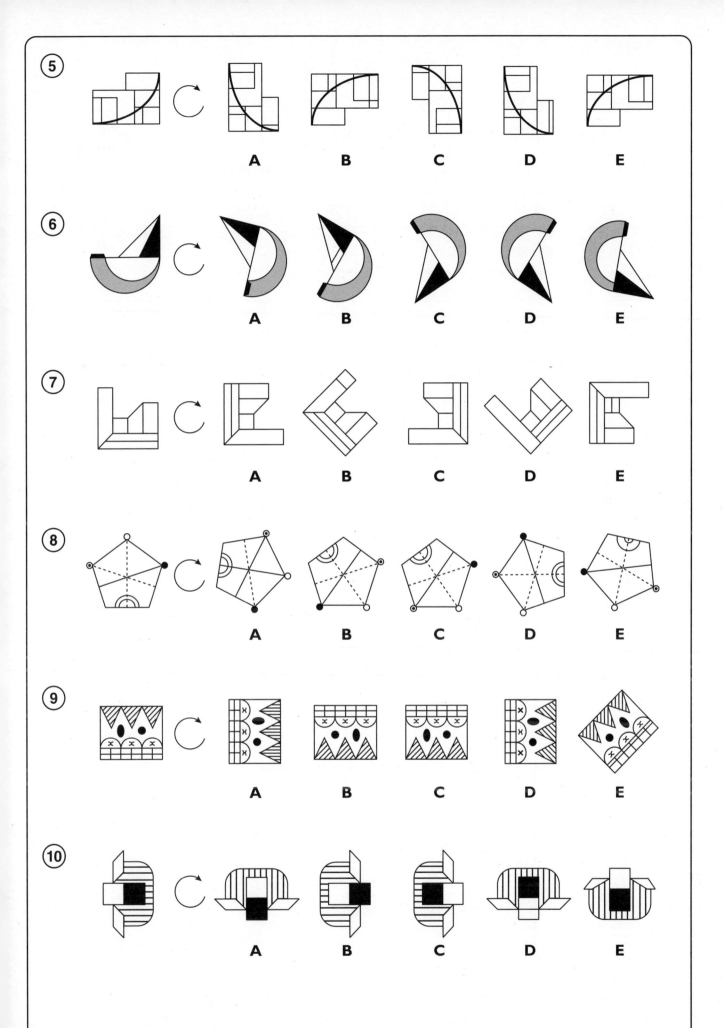

Test 18

You have 5 minutes to complete this test.

You have 10 questions to complete within the given time.

Decide which group of blocks could be used to make the figure shown on the left and circle the letter below it.

EXAMPLE

A B C Ⓓ E

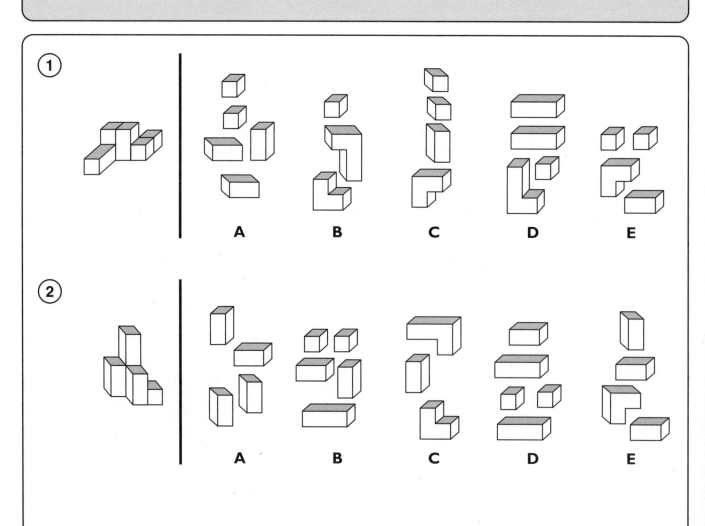

1

A B C D E

2

A B C D E

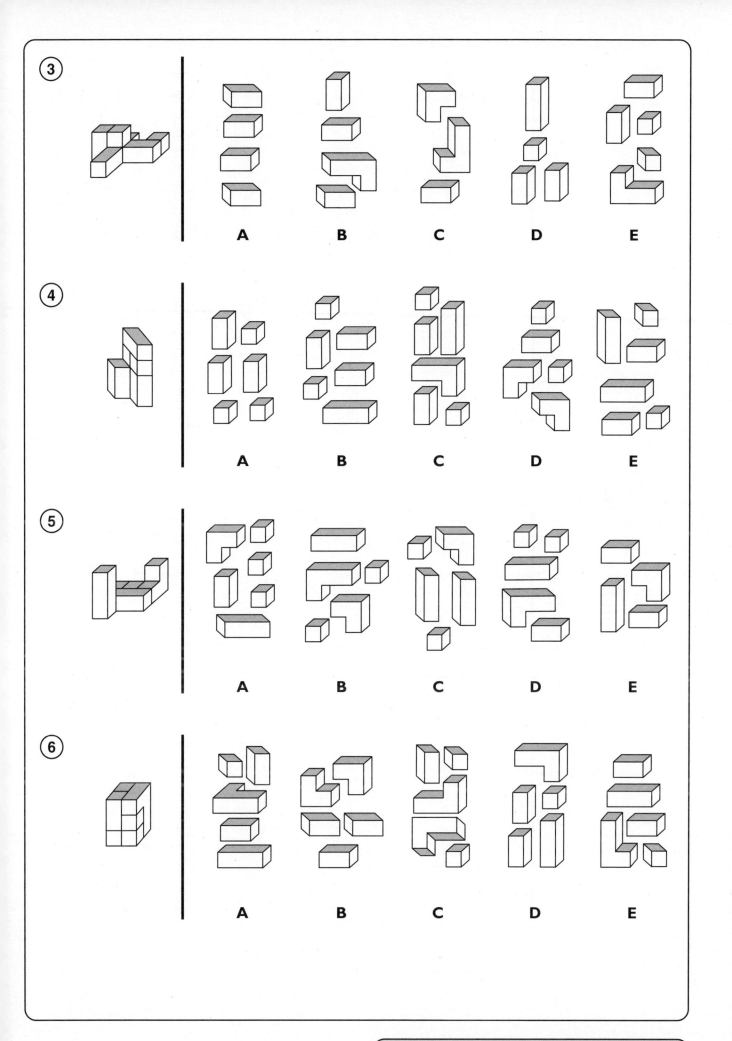

Questions continue on next page

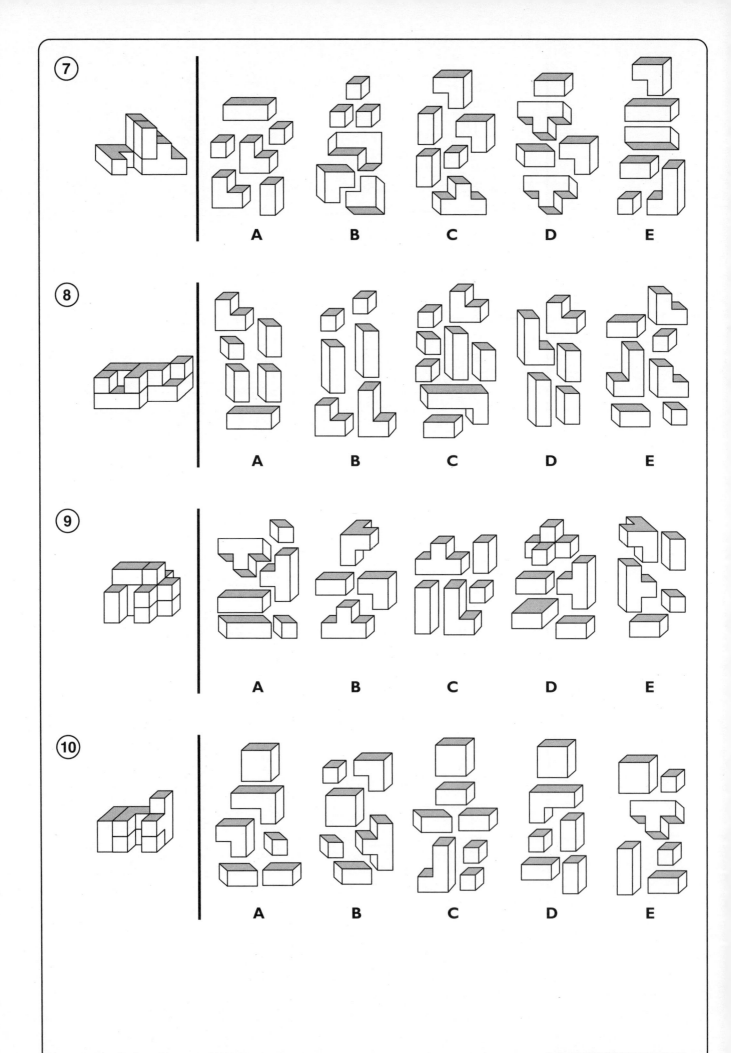

Test 19

You have 5 minutes to complete this test.

You have 10 questions to complete within the given time.

The shape on the left is hidden in one of the figures on the right. The shape does not change size. It may have been rotated but not reflected. Circle the letter below the figure that contains the hidden shape.

EXAMPLE

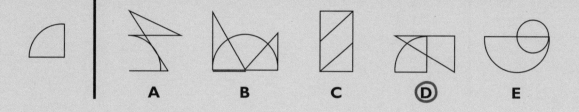

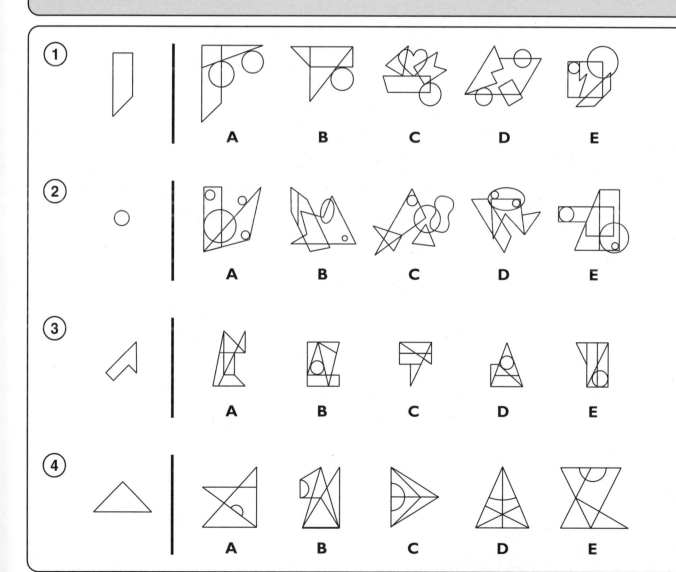

Questions continue on next page

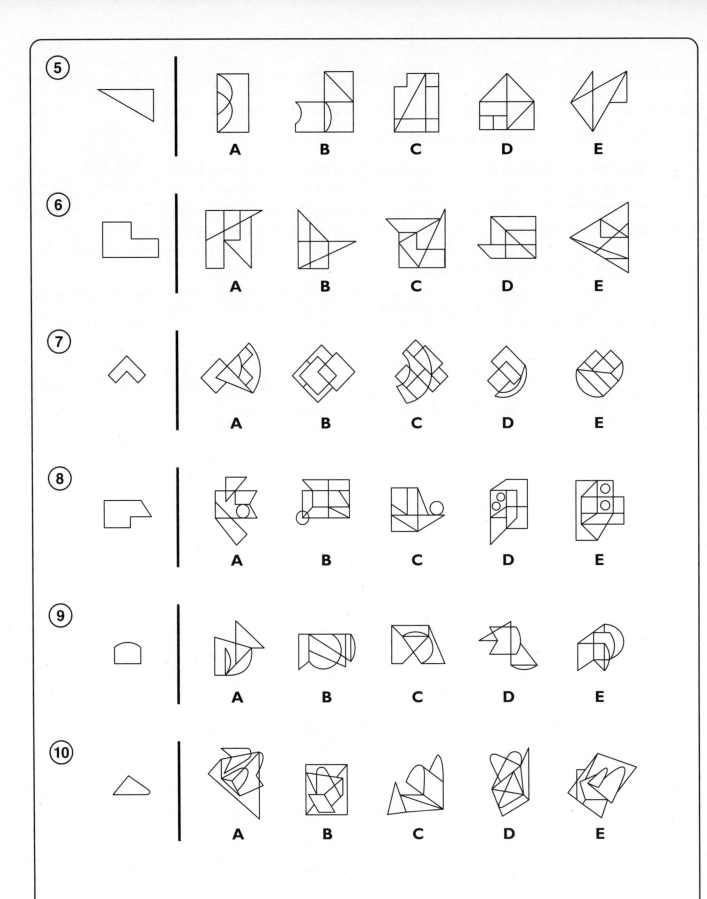

Test 20

You have 5 minutes to complete this test.

You have 10 questions to complete within the given time.

Look at the paper on the left. The paper will be folded along the dashed lines. Decide which figure shows what the paper will look like after it has been folded and circle the letter below it.

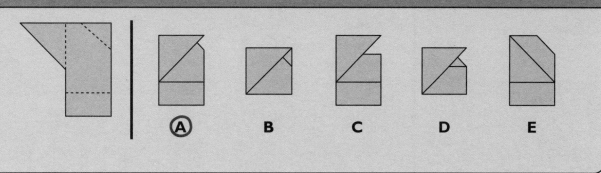

A   B   C   D   E

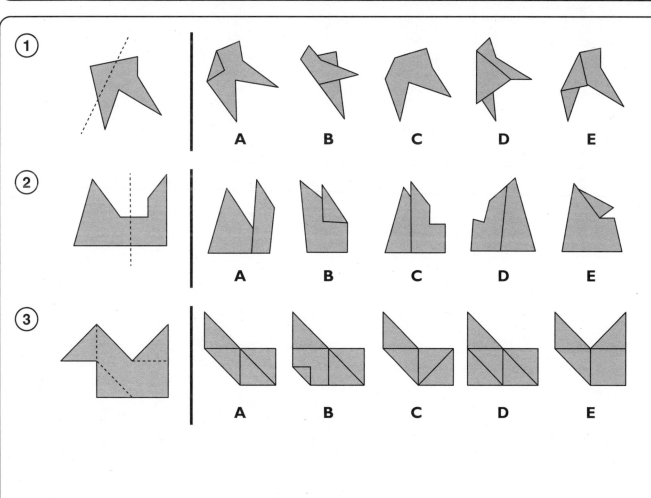

Questions continue on next page

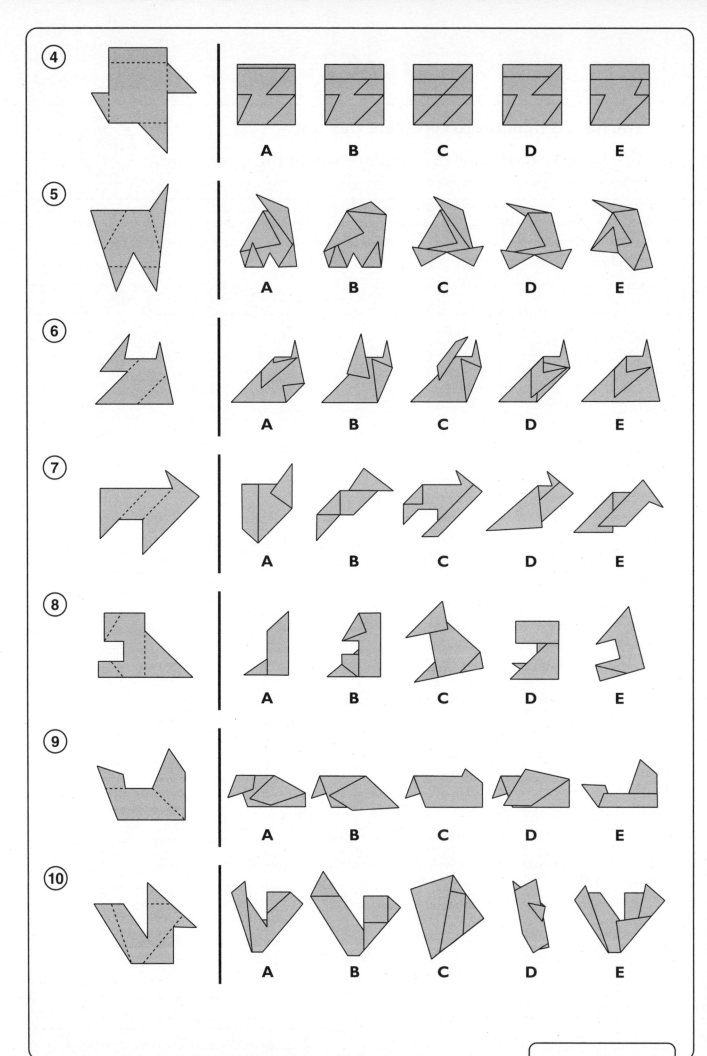

Score: .... / 10

Test 21

You have 5 minutes to complete this test.

You have 10 questions to complete within the given time.

Look at the cube on the left. Decide which figure shows the net that could be used to make the cube and circle the letter below it.

EXAMPLE

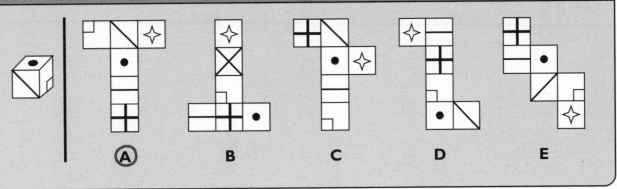

1

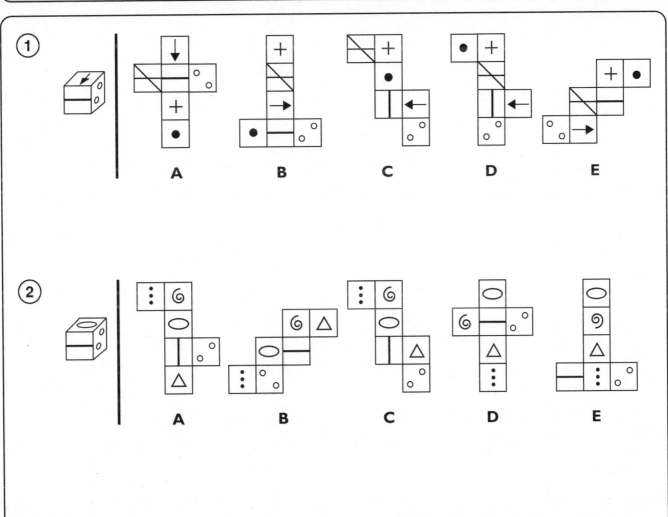

2

Questions continue on next page

51

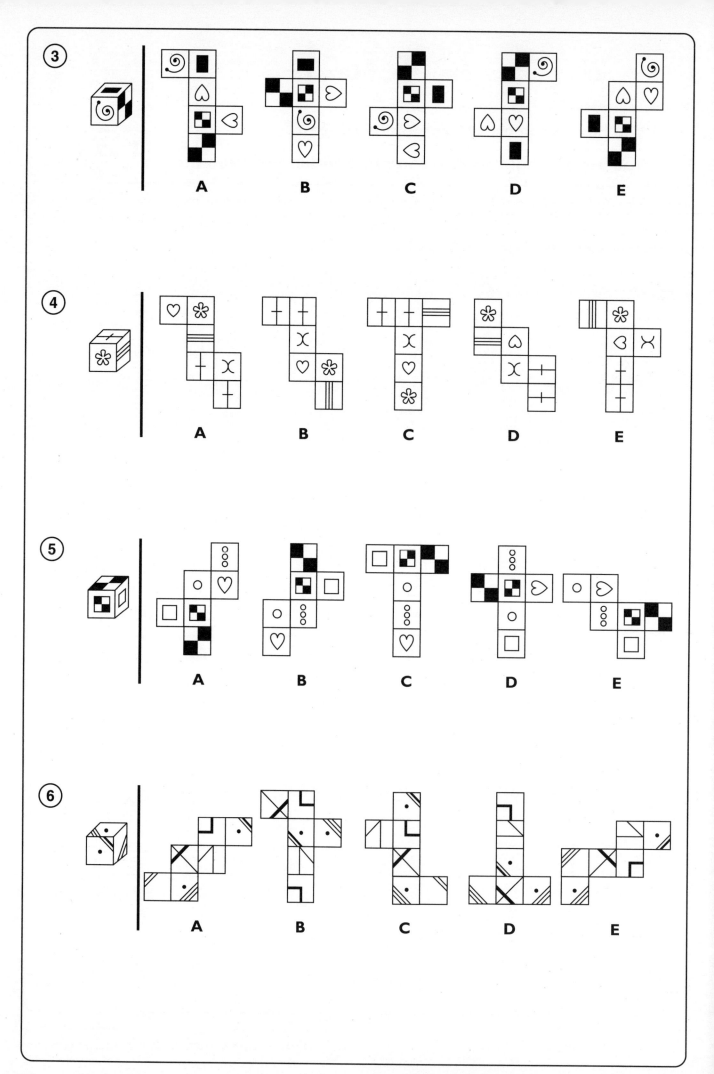

3

4

5

6

A B C D E

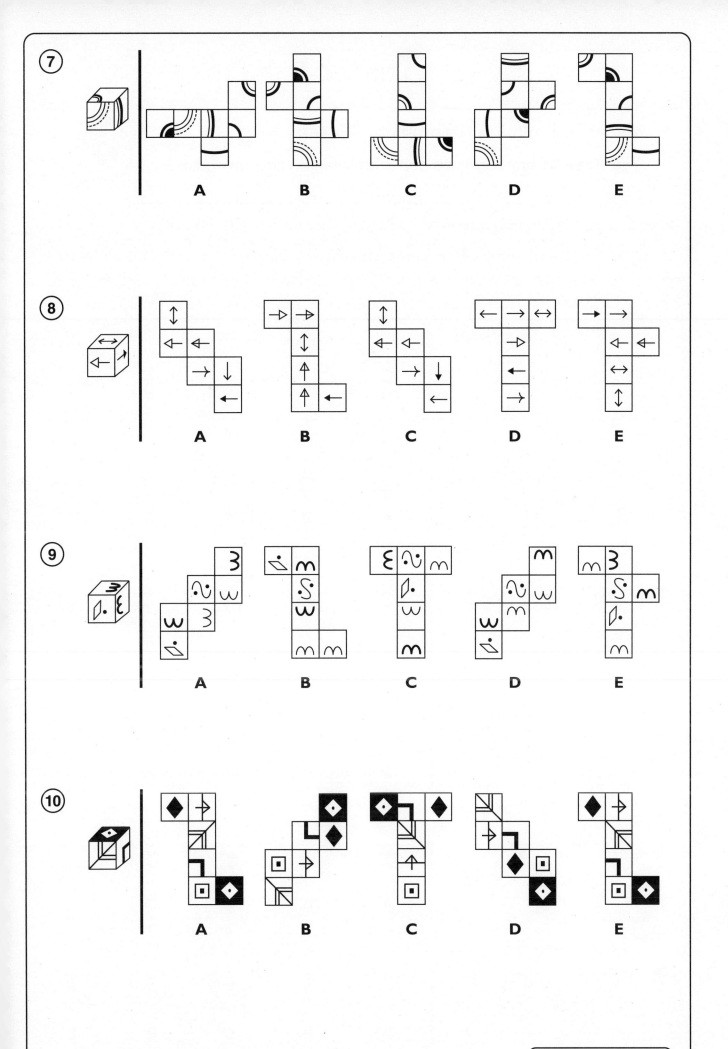

Test 22

You have 6 minutes to complete this test.

You have 12 questions to complete within the given time.

In each question, there is a sequence of triangles with one left empty.

Decide which triangle on the right completes the sequence and circle the letter below it.

EXAMPLE

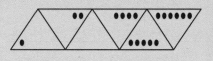

Ⓐ B C D E

①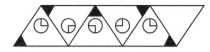

A B C D E

②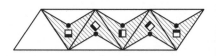

A B C D E

③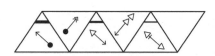

A B C D E

④

A B C D E

⑤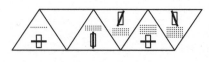

A B C D E

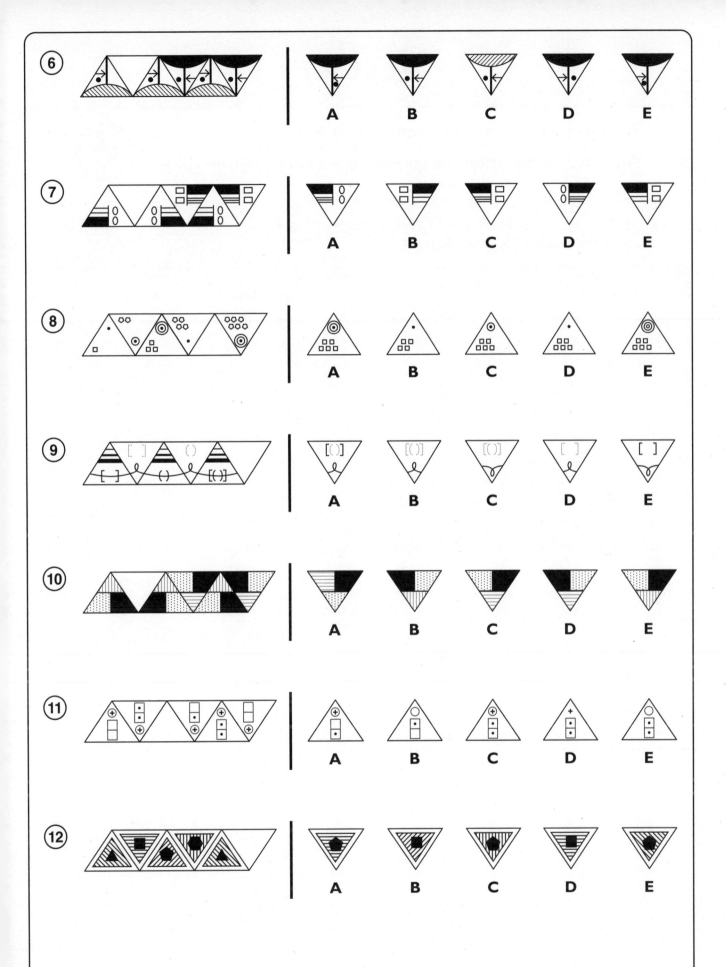

Test 23

Look at figures **A** and **B**. They are then rotated. Match the two rotations shown below to each of the original figures **A** and **B**.

EXAMPLE

A   B

A   Ⓑ

Ⓐ   B

Match the rotations shown in questions 1–5 to one of the original figures A, B, C, D or E.

A   B   C   D   E

①   A   B   C   D   E

②   A   B   C   D   E

③   A   B   C   D   E

④   A   B   C   D   E

⑤   A   B   C   D   E

Questions continue on next page

Match the rotations shown in questions 6–10 to one of the original figures A, B, C, D or E.

 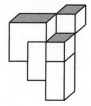 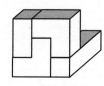

A   B   C   D   E

(6)   A   B   C   D   E

(7)   A   B   C   D   E

(8)   A   B   C   D   E

(9)   A   B   C   D   E

(10)   A   B   C   D   E

Score: .... / 10

58

Test 24

You have 6 minutes to complete this test.

You have 12 questions to complete within the given time.

In each grid, one square has been left empty.

Look at the five squares to the right. Decide which one completes the grid and circle the letter below it.

EXAMPLE

A	B	C	D	E

①

A   B   C   D   E

②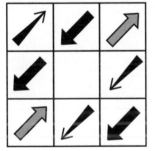

A   B   C   D   E

Questions continue on next page

59

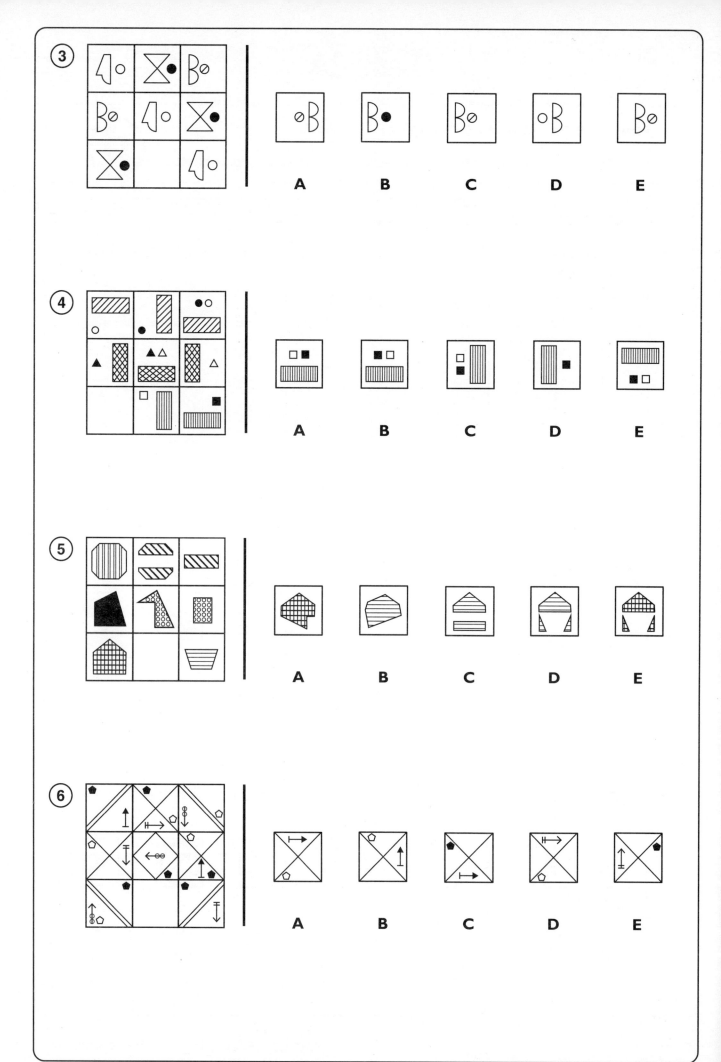

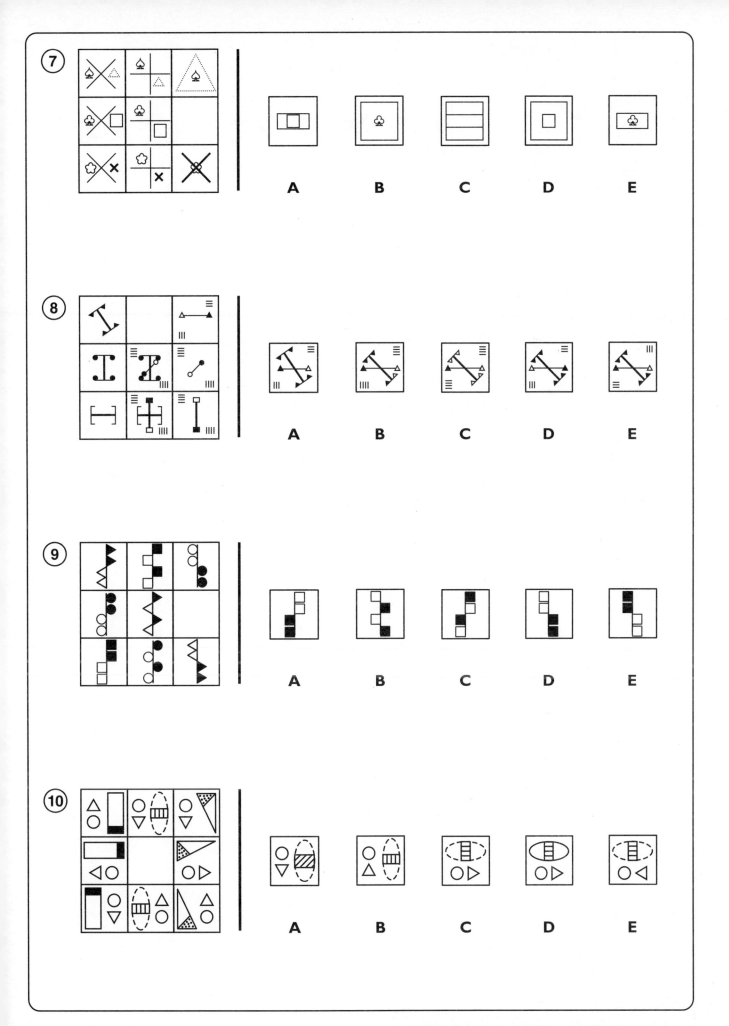

Questions continue on next page

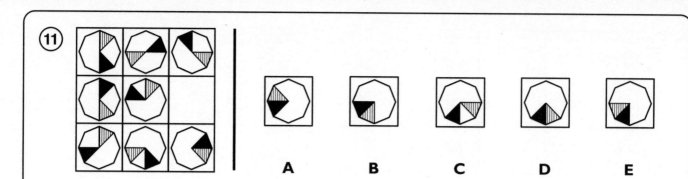

⑪

A B C D E

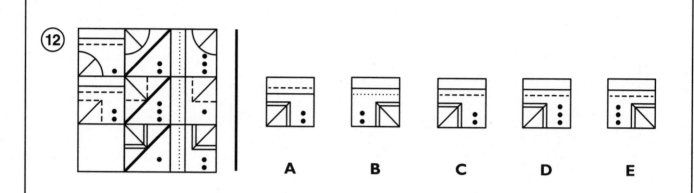

⑫

A B C D E

Answers

Test 1

Q1 C Moving from left to right, the shape is reflected in a horizontal mirror line. It gains small black dots along the right-hand side, internally. There are the same number of dots as there are sides of the shape. Therefore, the answer is C.

Q2 A Moving from left to right, the outer line of the figure becomes dotted. The overall figure is reflected in a vertical mirror line. The cross-hatched shading is changed to white. The white shading becomes striped vertically. Therefore, the answer is A.

Q3 A Moving from left to right, the arrow's direction changes by 180 degrees. The arrowhead changes from open to a closed triangle and is enlarged. The number of black dots increases by one. The arrow gains the same number of short perpendicular lines at the vacant end. Therefore, the answer is A.

Q4 D Moving from left to right, the whole figure is reflected in a vertical mirror line and the shading is rotated by 90 degrees. Therefore, the answer is D.

Q5 C Moving from left to right, the two separate curved lines are pushed together to make a complete circle. The left-hand small shape becomes enlarged and takes on the line type of the horizontal line at the bottom of the figure. It moves inside the circle. The right-hand small shape is shaded black and moved to the centre of the figure. Therefore, the answer is C.

Q6 E Moving from left to right, the shape becomes smaller, is duplicated, and the two small shapes are arranged vertically. The shapes overlap in the middle and the shading moves to the overlap. Therefore, the answer is E.

Q7 B Moving from left to right, the shape is duplicated, and the duplicated shape is rotated 180 degrees. The duplicated shape is emboldened and placed directly on top of the original shape. Therefore, the answer is B.

Q8 B Moving from left to right, the largest shape is rotated 180 degrees. The internal small shapes disappear and are replaced by black dots that overlap the largest shape. The number of small shapes is increased by one to give the number of black dots. Therefore, the answer is B.

Q9 E Moving from left to right, the small flag at the top of the figure is elongated, rotated 90 degrees clockwise and then reflected in a vertical mirror line. It is then placed at the right-hand side of the figure. The middle line remains unchanged. The two shapes arranged vertically on the left-hand side of the figure are elongated and placed one on top of the other. Therefore, the answer is E.

Q10 E Moving from left to right, the black and grey shading is swapped. The two styles of diagonal lines are swapped. The horizontal and vertical stripes are swapped. Therefore, the answer is E.

Test 2

Q1 D Moving from left to right in each row, the face of the 'bug' is rotated 180 degrees. The legs lose the dots of the 'feet' and a gap is introduced between the body and the legs. The number of legs remains consistent. Therefore, the answer is D.

Q2 A Moving from left to right in each row, the figure is rotated 45 degrees anticlockwise, and the double line is moved up to touch the angled line. The small shape below the double line moves to the top of the angled line. Therefore, the answer is A.

Q3 B Moving from left to right in each row, the large shield is made smaller, reflected in a horizontal mirror line and has additional perpendicular shading. The small white shape in the bottom left-hand corner is moved to the top right-hand corner and changed to black shading. Therefore, the answer is B.

Q4 B Moving from left to right in each row, the small double shape in the top left-hand corner has been changed to small black shapes at the end of each arrow. The arrows are made shorter and rotated 45 degrees anticlockwise. Therefore, the answer is B.

Q5 D Moving from left to right in each row, the two halves of the pointed oval move together and are rotated 90 degrees clockwise. The white triangle moves in front of the pointed oval. Therefore, the answer is D.

Q6 B Moving from left to right in each row, the large shape at the base of the figure is duplicated and placed at the top of each figure, with the two shapes touching vertically. The small middle figure becomes black-shaded and is moved to the lower left-hand corner of the figure. The two arrows are rotated 90 degrees clockwise and placed in the bottom right-hand corner of the figure. Therefore, the answer is B.

Q7 C Moving from left to right in each row, the large quadrilateral is rotated 90 degrees and the semicircle placed in the centre of the top side, with vertical lines extending down from either side of the semicircle to divide the shape. The semicircle gains black shading. The arrows are rotated 90 degrees and the arrowheads' direction swaps. The position of the arrows and quadrilateral moves: they each rotate one side clockwise around the figure. The small 'x' shape does not change style but is duplicated one each side of the black section. Therefore, the answer is C.

Q8 C Moving from left to right in each row, the long line with three short perpendicular lines crossing it rotates 90 degrees anticlockwise. The long line becomes fine, and the short lines become emboldened. The small line cutting off one corner of the figure moves one corner clockwise, and the small dot moves one corner anticlockwise. Therefore, the answer is C.

Q9 A Moving from left to right in each row, the bold shape is rotated 180 degrees but the small shapes inside it do not move. The long line behind the bold shape is rotated 90 degrees. The three small lines cutting off one corner of the figure move two corners clockwise. Therefore, the answer is A.

Q10 C Moving from left to right in each row, the arrows are rotated 90 degrees anticlockwise and one extra arrow is added. The broken lines behind the arrows reduce in number by half. Therefore, the answer is C.

Q11 C Moving from top to bottom in each column, the outside line type of the square becomes a single vertical line to the left of the figure. The evenly spaced dots are pushed towards each other and placed in the bottom right-hand corner of the figure. The large square is made smaller and positioned in the top right-hand corner of the figure, with the divisions kept. The divided shape that is placed in each section of the large square is made whole, and placed between the dots and the vertical line. Therefore, the answer is C.

Q12 A Moving from left to right in each row, the large divided shape with one bold side is reflected in a horizontal mirror line and moved to the bottom of the figure, and one more dividing line is added. The fine-lined shape moves from the bottom to the top of the figure and three small shapes are added in the scallops. These small shapes are the same as in the divided shape. Therefore, the answer is A.

Test 3

Q1 D Moving left to right along the sequence, the diagonal line alternates between bold and dashed. The circle alternates between dotted and solid. The shape in the bottom right-hand corner of the figure gains one side in each figure. Therefore, the answer is D.

Q2 D Moving left to right along the sequence, one square at a time gains a cross. In the next figure, that square becomes a circle. In the next square, it vanishes. In each figure, there is both a square with a cross and a circle replacing one square, so two steps are visible in each figure. Therefore, the answer is D.

Q3 E Moving left to right along the sequence, the bold side moves one place clockwise around the pentagon. The cross alternates between bottom left and top right of the pentagon. The circle moves one place anticlockwise round the pentagon. Therefore, the answer is E.

Q4 D Moving left to right along the sequence, the small shape moves one corner clockwise in each figure and alternates between triangle and circle. The short diagonal line becomes bolder in each figure and rotates in line with the small shape. The shading alternates in turn: horizontal lines, vertical lines, cross-hatched lines. Therefore, the answer is D.

Q5 C Moving left to right along the sequence, the triangles alternate between equilateral and isosceles. The short horizontal line moves lower in each figure. The arrow moves one side anticlockwise in each figure. The arrowheads alternate in turn: black, white and double. Therefore, the answer is C.

Q6 C Moving left to right along the sequence, each shape is in the bottom position for two figures, with cross-hatched shading each time. In turn, they are triangles, squares and isosceles trapezia. The upper shapes swap places in each pair of figures with a consistent bottom shape. The shading remains consistent for each shape's position. Therefore, the answer is C.

Q7 B Moving left to right along the sequence, the hearts alternate between black and white. In each figure, one additional circle is added to the bottom left of the figure, which pushes the shaded circles along one position to the right. Therefore, the answer is B.

Q8 B Moving left to right along the sequence, the number of loops increases by one in each figure. The figures alternate between having a black dot and not. Therefore, the answer is B.

Q9 **E** Moving left to right along the sequence, the shading moves one section higher each time. Therefore, the answer is E.

Q10 **C** Moving left to right along the sequence, the bold arrow moves one side clockwise in each figure. The fine arrow moves one side anticlockwise in each figure. The two circles alternate between black and white overlapping. Therefore, the answer is C.

Test 4

Q1 **A** In each figure on the left of the question, there is one long fine line and four bold lines (two longer, and two shorter). None of the lines are parallel. The bold lines need to cross over three times. Therefore, the answer is A.

Q2 **E** In each figure on the left of the question, there is a large shape, with a smaller version overlapping it. The overlap is shaded black. The small shape is always aligned at the top of the large shape. Therefore, the answer is E.

Q3 **E** In each figure on the left of the question, there is a clockwise arrow with an arrowhead of the same open style. Therefore, the answer is E.

Q4 **A** In each figure on the left of the question, there is a large semicircle with six small scallops, with a straight line below. The straight line has an identical small shape at either end. If the figures were rotated in the same way, the white circle would be in the same position relative to the bold line. Therefore, the answer is A.

Q5 **B** In each figure on the left of the question, there is a triangle at the top, a smaller shape in the middle, and a larger shape at the bottom. The middle shape has diagonal shading from the bottom left to the top right. Therefore, the answer is B.

Q6 **D** In each figure on the left of the question, there is a white shape divided with a bold line. Behind it, there is a larger striped shape with a double border. The direction of the striped shading is perpendicular to the direction of the bold line. Therefore, the answer is D.

Q7 **D** In each figure on the left of the question, there is one fewer black dot than there is scallop. There is a small square inside the large shape, and a small triangle outside the shape positioned alongside the small square either side of the large shape. Therefore, the answer is D.

Q8 **B** In each figure on the left of the question, there is a circle divided into equal sections. Two are shaded, the upper of which is vertically striped and the lower of which is horizontally striped.

Around the edge of the circle, there is a large shape with the same number of sides as there are divisions. Therefore, the answer is B.

Q9 **A** In each figure on the left of the question, there is a large square, divided in half. One half is shaded, and there is a parallel bold line running alongside the shaded half. There is an arrow crossing through the square through the white half. Therefore, the answer is A.

Q10 **A** In each figure on the left of the question, the arrow originates from the black shape. Therefore, the answer is A.

Test 5

Q1 **D** KW

N = the bold line crosses the shape in two places
K = the bold line crosses the shape in one place
Q = the bold line is inside the shape and does not cross it
B = quadrilateral
H = hexagon
W = pentagon

Therefore, the answer is KW.

Q2 **E** PW

N = black inner circle
I = white inner circle
P = grey inner circle
W = horizontal dividing line
D = vertical dividing line
O = diagonal dividing line, top left to bottom right
E = diagonal dividing line, top right to bottom left

Therefore, the answer is PW.

Q3 **B** WP

S = rectangle divided into two sections
V = rectangle divided into three sections
W = rectangle divided into four sections
P = same number of dots as sections
Q = different number of dots than sections

Therefore, the answer is WP.

Q4 **B** HO

J = shading not adjacent to left-hand side of figure
H = shading adjacent to left-hand side of figure
M = cross-hatching
A = vertical shading
N = horizontal shading
O = dotted shading

Therefore, the answer is HO.

Q5 **D** ZB

A = outer and inner shapes are the same
B = outer and inner shapes are different
Z = rectangle with cut-out corners as the outer shape
Y = arrow as the outer shape
X = club as the outer shape
W = diamond as the outer shape

Therefore, the answer is ZB.

Q6 **C** MR

K = black dot above the triangles
M = black dot to the left of the triangles
L = black dot to the bottom of the triangles
T = 5 triangles
S = 4 triangles
R = 6 triangles

Therefore, the answer is MR.

Q7 **A** AP

A = same number of small shapes as lobes on the cloud
B = different number of small shapes than lobes on the cloud
D = cloud in top left-hand corner
P = cloud in bottom left-hand corner
G = cloud in bottom right-hand corner

Therefore, the answer is AP.

Q8 **A** FZ

F = bold line in front of the right angle
G = bold line behind the right angle
D = solid lined right angle
A = dotted lined right angle
Z = dashed lined right angle

Therefore, the answer is FZ.

Q9 **C** RT

V = if the bold dotted line were positioned vertically, the missing circle would be in the bottom left-hand corner
R = if the bold dotted line were positioned vertically, the missing circle would be in the top left-hand corner
Y = if the bold dotted line were positioned vertically, the missing circle would be in the top right-hand corner
L = circles are black
U = circles are solid white
T = circles are transparent

Therefore, the answer is RT.

Q10 **E** HG

X = short vertical line is on the top left-hand side of the horizontal lines

H = short vertical line is on the middle right of the horizontal lines
N = short vertical line is on the bottom left of the horizontal lines
Q = short vertical line is on the middle left of the horizontal lines
G = circle is overlapping a horizontal line
M = circle is between horizontal lines

Therefore, the answer is HG.

Test 6

Q1 **E** In all the other figures, the bold lines are parallel and the fine lines are not parallel. Therefore, the answer is E.

Q2 **A** In all other figures, if the circles are on the left of the line, the white circle is below the black circle. If the circles are on the right of the line, the white circle is above the black circle. Therefore, the answer is A.

Q3 **A** All the other figures have a vertical line of symmetry. Therefore, the answer is A.

Q4 **C** In all the other figures, the small, black-shaded shapes are on the left. Therefore, the answer is C.

Q5 **D** All the other figures have alternating small shapes down the outside columns. Therefore, the answer is D.

Q6 **A** In all the other figures, the black shape is uppermost as the shapes are placed on top of one another. Therefore, the answer is A.

Q7 **E** In all the other figures, starting with the rectangle and moving clockwise around the circle, the components are rectangle, then arrow with solid arrowhead, then arrow with fine arrowhead. Therefore, the answer is E.

Q8 **D** In all the other figures, there are five components. Therefore, the answer is D.

Q9 **D** In all the other figures, the top rectangle is made up of the shading from the bottom two rectangles overlapping. Therefore, the answer is D.

Q10 **B** In all the other figures, the arrow points to the straight side of the semicircle. Therefore, the answer is B.

Test 7

Q1 **A** In the figures on the left-hand side, each polygon has a smaller version of the same shape overlapping. The small polygon is shaded black on the outside where it overlaps the larger polygon. There is also a small overlapping triangle and circle, which are shaded black inside the larger polygon. Therefore, the answer is A.

Q2 A In the figures on the left-hand side, the oval is divided into an even number of slices. The number of horizontal lines under the oval is the same as half the number of divided slices. To the right of the oval, there is a square joined to the oval by a short horizontal line. Therefore, the answer is A.

Q3 D In the figures on the left-hand side, there is a large triangle with another shape overlapping the bottom left-hand corner. To the top right of the triangle, there is a small black shape that is the same as the shape formed by the two overlapping shapes. Therefore, the answer is D.

Q4 C In the figures on the left-hand side, the arrow on the left points down and the arrow on the right points upwards; the dot is on the left of the figure. Therefore, the answer is C.

Q5 E In the figures on the left-hand side, there are two semicircles and two arrows. The black arrow points towards the black semicircle, into the square, and the open arrow points away from the white semicircle, out of the square. The white semicircle bulges out of the square and the black semicircle pushes into the square. Therefore, the answer is E.

Q6 D In the figures on the left-hand side, there is a bold line and a fine line that are perpendicular to one another inside a circle. On the right-hand side of the circle, there is a small crescent moon with the points to the right-hand side of it. Therefore, the answer is D.

Q7 C In the figures on the left-hand side, there is a small shape surrounded by a larger shape. The larger shape has one side more than the smaller shape. Therefore, the answer is C.

Q8 A In the figures on the left-hand side, there are black dots and white circles. There are always two black dots. Therefore, the answer is A.

Q9 A In the figures on the left-hand side, there is a shape with black dots and short parallel lines in it. There are always two black dots. The dots combined with the number of lines totals the number of sides of the large shape. Therefore, the answer is A.

Q10 E In the figures on the left-hand side, there is a black arrow with a wiggly line. The line has two loops. There are two black stars, one each side of the arrow's line. Therefore, the answer is E.

Test 8

Q1 C YXS

X = 3 small black shapes the same as one another
B = 3 small black shapes different from one another
S = flag points left
D = flag points right
P = flag has one point
Y = flag has three points
O = flag has two points

Therefore, the answer is YXS.

Q2 B HWZ

P = rectangle in bottom left-hand corner
H = square in bottom left-hand corner
T = triangle in bottom left-hand corner
W = circle in top left-hand corner
N = no circle in top left-hand corner
Q = rectangle on right-hand side
Z = line on right-hand side

Therefore, the answer is HWZ.

Q3 A QP

F = bottom triangle is grey
N = bottom triangle is striped
Q = bottom triangle has crosses
T = top triangle is black
P = top triangle has dots
W = top triangle is white

Therefore, the answer is QP.

Q4 A OG

T = 8 scallops
O = 7 scallops
N = arrow points to top left-hand corner
G = arrow points to bottom right-hand corner

Therefore, the answer is OG.

Q5 E AWY

V = 3 loops
W = 4 loops
Z = circle has a black centre
Y = circle has a white centre
A = square with a cross in
B = striped square
C = bold striped square

Therefore, the answer is AWY.

Q6 B KYO

K = 2 black circles, 1 white
N = 2 white circles, 1 black
R = 1 striped circle, 2 white
Z = hexagon
Y = pentagon
O = black stripe
P = white stripe

Therefore, the answer is KYO.

Q7 **B** ZOE

M = white square on right-hand side
H = white square in middle
Z = white square on left-hand side
W = rectangle in middle
R = rectangle on left-hand side
O = rectangle on right-hand side
E = rectangle has cross-hatching
D = rectangle has stripes

Therefore, the answer is ZOE.

Q8 **C** PIR

J = inner shading is diagonal stripes
P = no inner shading
L = outer and inner shapes the same as one another
I = outer and inner shapes different from one another
Q = outer shape is bold
R = outer shape is not bold

Therefore, the answer is PIR.

Q9 **D** PW

D = bold circle
P = fine circle
E = double circle
U = quadrilateral
V = hexagon
W = pentagon

Therefore, the answer is PW.

Q10 **C** ZEB

Z = large size shape
A = small size shape
P = triangle
E = trapezium
B = circle below other shape
C = circle above other shape

Therefore, the answer is ZEB.

Test 9

Q1	C	Q2	B
Q3	E	Q4	A
Q5	A	Q6	D
Q7	A	Q8	D
Q9	C	Q10	C

Test 10

Q1 **D** Starting in the top left-hand corner, and moving from left to right across each row, the dot alternates from bottom to top in each rectangle. The bold line moves one side clockwise. Therefore, the answer is D.

Q2 **C** The long lines are continuous across the hexagonal grid and 'flow' between each mini hexagon. The arrows point alternately left and right in each row of the hexagon. Therefore, the answer is C.

Q3 **A** The shapes diagonally opposite one another are identical. The bold lines are all at the central outer edge of each mini hexagon. Moving anticlockwise around the outer mini hexagons, starting in the top left-hand corner, the circles get larger each time. Therefore, the answer is A.

Q4 **B** The lines in the mini hexagons diagonally opposite one another are reflected. The number of circles increases by one each time, starting in the mini hexagon in the centre left of the figure. Therefore, the answer is B.

Q5 **B** Starting in the top left-hand mini hexagon, the small shapes move two triangles clockwise in each subsequent hexagon, working across each row from left to right. Therefore, the answer is B.

Q6 **E** In diagonal rows from top right to bottom left, each figure is identical. Therefore, the answer is E.

Q7 **A** Figures diagonally opposite one another are identical. Therefore, the answer is A.

Q8 **C** Moving clockwise around the edge of the grid: the arrow alternates between vertical and horizontal; the number of dots is sequenced 1, 2, 3; the position of the striped triangle moves one side clockwise; the stripes alternate between vertical and both diagonals; the parallel lines move two sides clockwise in each hexagon. Therefore, the answer is C.

Q9 **D** All of the long lines are continuous across the hexagonal grid and 'flow' between each mini hexagon. The black triangles follow a diagonal pattern from top left to bottom right (three in the first diagonal column, then two, then one). The top row has small squares and one white triangle in each mini hexagon, the middle row has small ovals and two white triangles, and the last row has small rectangles and three white triangles in each mini hexagon. Therefore, the answer is D.

Q10 **E** In diagonal rows from top left to bottom right, each figure is identical. Therefore, the answer is E.

Test 11

Q1 **A** Moving around the outside of the star, each triangle has two small triangles: one black and one with a circle. Around the edge of the star, these small triangles alternate. Crossing through the middle of the star, each straight line of triangles has the same central shape. Therefore, the answer is A.

Q2 C Crossing through the middle of the star, each straight line of triangles has alternate shading. The inner triangles all have two squares aligned with one another. Therefore, the answer is C.

Q3 B Moving around the outside of the star, the pentagons' upper antennae alternate in the direction they point. The number of dots alternates between 1, 2 and 3. The shading is the same for opposite pentagons across the star grid. Therefore, the answer is B.

Q4 A Crossing through the middle of the star, each straight line of triangles has the same shape rotated 180 degrees between each triangle. Therefore, the answer is A.

Q5 A Moving from each outer triangle to the inner triangle it touches, the crosses turn to black ovals and the white circles do not change. Therefore, the answer is A.

Q6 E Moving around the inner triangles of the star, the figures alternate between a square and a triangle. Each figure has a black-shaded inner shape, then a solid black line, then a dashed black line. Therefore, the answer is E.

Q7 D Crossing through the middle of the star, each straight line of triangles has an identical figure in the two outer triangles. Therefore, the answer is D.

Q8 B Moving from the inside triangle to each outside triangle next to it, the inner shape is a mirror image of the outer shape, reflected in the line that divides them. The inner triangle has a dotted or dashed line on the outside of a black-shaded figure, whereas the outer triangle has a solid outline with the same type of dashed or dotted line inside it. Therefore, the answer is B.

Q9 C The star is divided in two horizontally, with each half made up of three upper triangles and three lower triangles. Moving from upper to lower triangles, the shape stays the same. However, in each upper triangle there is one bold figure; in each lower triangle there are two overlapping fine figures of the same shape. Therefore, the answer is C.

Q10 C Moving around the inner triangles of the star, the circles alternate between two overlapping or three overlapping. The V-shapes are always arranged on the sides touching the outside triangle. Therefore, the answer is C.

Q11 D Crossing through the middle of the star, each straight line of triangles has the same shape of arrow, which rotates 45 degrees clockwise (moving from top to bottom of each straight line). Therefore, the answer is D.

Q12 B There is a vertical line of symmetry through the middle of the star. Each figure in the star appears twice, and therefore the line and circle should be identical to the figure below the missing triangle, and the straight lines in the corners should be in the top two corners to continue the pattern with the adjoining corners. Therefore, the answer is B.

Test 12

Q1 E Moving from the left triangle to the right triangle, the figures are rotated 90 degrees clockwise. Therefore, the answer is E.

Q2 B Moving from the left triangle to the right triangle, the black and white shading swaps position, and the circle which is positioned in front of the other two moves to be positioned behind the other two. Therefore, the answer is B.

Q3 B Moving from the left triangle to the right triangle, the figures are rotated 45 degrees clockwise and emboldened. Therefore, the answer is B.

Q4 D Moving from the left triangle to the right triangle, the circles move outwards, each to a corner of the triangle. In the triangles pointing upwards, the uppermost circle moves to the top corner, the middle circle moves to the bottom left corner and the bottom circle moves to the bottom right corner. Therefore, the answer is D.

Q5 A Moving from the left triangle to the right triangle, the stars double in number and change to crosses. The crosses move outside the sector. The sector gains the same number of stripes as there were stars, and the direction of the stripe matches the direction of the original striped shading. Therefore, the answer is A.

Q6 D Moving from the left triangle to the right triangle, the two dashed sides of each figure are removed, and the double side remains. The outer double side is changed to become dashed. Therefore, the answer is D.

Q7 D Moving from the left triangle to the right triangle, the heart's shading rotates 45 degrees clockwise and the semicircle below turns 180 degrees. Therefore, the answer is D.

Q8 B Moving from the left triangle to the right triangle, the arrowhead doubles and they are positioned vertically on top of one another. A short vertical line is added each side of the arrowheads. At the top of the triangle is a sector, which changes shading moving from the left to the right-hand triangle. Therefore, the answer is B.

Q9 D Moving from the left triangle to the right triangle, the direction of the triangle and semicircle in each component section indicates the direction of the triangular line and the scalloped line. If a semicircle or triangle points upwards in the left-hand triangle, the scallops or zigzags will be upwards on the right-hand triangle. If a semicircle or triangle points downwards in the left-hand triangle, the scallops or zigzags point downwards in the right-hand triangle. Plain black squares turn to fine dotted lines. Therefore, the answer is D.

Q10 C Moving from the left triangle to the right triangle, the dotted line types swap with the bold lines and the dashed lines do not change. The position of the lines does not change. Therefore, the answer is C.

Q11 D Moving from the left triangle to the right triangle, the scalloped line and the straight line swap position, and the scalloped line rotates 180 degrees. Therefore, the answer is D.

Q12 B Moving from the left triangle to the right triangle, the number of triangles matches the number of short perpendicular lines on the corresponding arrow. The shading of the triangles matches the shading of the arrowhead on the corresponding arrow. The triangles point in the same direction as the corresponding arrow. Therefore, the answer is B.

Test 13

Q1	A	Q2	E
Q3	A	Q4	B
Q5	D	Q6	E
Q7	C	Q8	B
Q9	C	Q10	D

Test 14

Q1	B	Q2	D
Q3	B	Q4	C
Q5	B	Q6	A
Q7	E	Q8	A
Q9	E	Q10	C

Test 15

Q1	E	Q2	D
Q3	D	Q4	C
Q5	C	Q6	E
Q7	E	Q8	D
Q9	B	Q10	D
Q11	A	Q12	D

Test 16

Q1	D	Q2	A
Q3	B	Q4	D
Q5	E	Q6	C
Q7	B	Q8	B
Q9	C	Q10	A

Test 17

Q1	E	Q2	E
Q3	E	Q4	C
Q5	E	Q6	D
Q7	C	Q8	B
Q9	B	Q10	C

Test 18

Q1	A	Q2	B
Q3	E	Q4	D
Q5	C	Q6	C
Q7	D	Q8	E
Q9	D	Q10	B

Test 19

Q1 B

Q2 E

Q3 A

Q4 C

Q5 C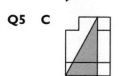

Q6 A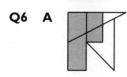

Q7 A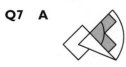

Q8 B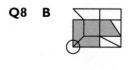

Q9 E

Q10 D

Test 20

Q1	E		Q2	C
Q3	A		Q4	B
Q5	A		Q6	D
Q7	E		Q8	B
Q9	B		Q10	A

Test 21

Q1	C		Q2	D
Q3	E		Q4	B
Q5	A		Q6	C
Q7	A		Q8	C
Q9	D		Q10	E

Test 22

Q1 A Moving from left to right across the sequence, the shaded corner of the triangles moves one corner clockwise in each figure. The right-angle in the circle rotates 90 degrees clockwise in each figure. Therefore, the answer is A.

Q2 D Moving from left to right across the sequence, the square rotates 45 degrees clockwise in each figure. The arrowhead alternates between pointing upward and downward and the diagonal striped shading remains consistent across each figure. Therefore, the answer is D.

Q3 E Moving from left to right across the sequence, the triangles pointing upwards have a bold line at the top that decreases in width in each figure. The figures' arrows come in pairs: firstly, each upward pointing triangle has an arrow; then the downward pointing triangle afterwards features the same arrow but rotated 90 degrees clockwise; the upper figure on the arrow is then doubled. Therefore, the answer is E.

Q4 D Moving from left to right across the sequence, the hexagons come in trios (three white, followed by three black). The number of small circles arranged vertically follows the pattern 1, 2, 3 and then repeats. The circles are to the right of the white hexagons and to the left of the black hexagons. Therefore, the answer is D.

Q5 E Moving from left to right across the sequence, the rectangle is intersected by a bold line that rotates 45 degrees clockwise in each figure. The number of dotted horizontal lines increases by one in each figure. Therefore, the answer is E.

Q6 B All of the upward pointing triangles are identical and all of the downward pointing triangles are identical. Therefore, the answer is B.

Q7 C Moving from left to right across the sequence, the upward pointing triangles are identical but alternating mirror images of one another. The downward pointing triangles are identical but alternating mirror images of one another. Therefore, the answer is C.

Q8 C Moving from left to right across the sequence, the number of rings around the dot is 0, 1, 2, 0, 1, 2. The number of small, repeated shapes increases by one each time. All of the downward pointing triangles have small pentagons. All of the upward pointing triangles have small squares. Therefore, the answer is C.

Q9 B Moving from left to right across the sequence, the brackets are repeated from each upward pointing triangle in the downward pointing triangle next to it, but in dotted lines rather than solid. Across all the triangles flows a curved 'ribbon' shape. Only the upward pointing triangles have bold lines at the top. Therefore, the answer is B.

Q10 **D** Moving from left to right across the sequence, the upward pointing triangles are identical but alternating mirror images of one another. The downward pointing triangles are identical but alternating mirror images of one another. Therefore, the answer is D.

Q11 **A** Moving from left to right across the sequence, the dots in the squares follow the pattern 0, 2, 1, 1, 2, 0. The circle with a plus sign alternates between the top and the bottom of the triangles, and the squares are consistent in every figure of the sequence. Therefore, the answer is A.

Q12 **D** Moving from left to right across the sequence, each small black figure gains one side until there is a small hexagon, before returning to a triangle. The diagonal striped shading rotates by 45 degrees anticlockwise each time. Therefore, the answer is D.

Test 23

Q1	**A**	**Q2**	**E**
Q3	**B**	**Q4**	**C**
Q5	**D**	**Q6**	**B**
Q7	**D**	**Q8**	**E**
Q9	**A**	**Q10**	**C**

Test 24

Q1 **C** Working in diagonals (from bottom left to top right) the style and direction of arrows remain consistent. Therefore, the answer is C.

Q2 **A** Moving from left to right in each row, the large striped shape becomes finer and shaded black in the third column. The small shape remains fine, is enlarged and is placed overlapping the black shape in the third column. Therefore, the answer is A.

Q3 **C** Working in diagonals (from top left to bottom right), the figures are identical. Therefore, the answer is C.

Q4 **E** Moving from left to right along each row, the rectangle moves one side clockwise. The shading itself does not rotate. In each row, there is one small white shape, one small black shape, and one pair of black and white shapes. In the pairs, the small black shape is always on the left-hand side. Therefore, the answer is E.

Q5 **D** The figure in the first column is made up of the figures in the second and third columns combined. The shading of the figures in the middle column is the same as the shading in

the third column, for figures in each row. Therefore, the answer is D.

Q6 **A** In each column and row of the grid, each of the three different arrows appears once. In each row, the direction of the arrow rotates 90 degrees clockwise each time. The squares at the corners of the grid each have a double diagonal line and the squares between have a large central cross. In each row of the grid, there is a square with a black pentagon, one with a white pentagon and one with both a black and a white pentagon. Therefore, the answer is A.

Q7 **B** Moving from left to right, the third shape in each row contains the two small shapes from the first two columns, one inside the other. The shape on the right-hand side of the first square in the row becomes enlarged and then the outer shape. The left-hand small shape remains the same size and is positioned centrally within the large shape. Therefore, the answer is B.

Q8 **A** The middle column is composed of the figures from the right-hand column overlapped with the figures from the left-hand column (working along each row horizontally). The colour swaps in the small shapes at either end of the line when the figures are overlapped. Therefore, the answer is A.

Q9 **D** Working in diagonal lines (from top left to bottom right), the type of shape in each figure is consistent. In each column, the position of the shading is consistent. Therefore, the answer is D.

Q10 **C** Moving down each column, the entire figure is rotated 90 degrees anticlockwise. Therefore, the answer is C.

Q11 **E** Moving from left to right along each row, the black sector of the octagon moves two-eighths anticlockwise and the striped sector of the octagon moves three-eighths anticlockwise. Therefore, the answer is E.

Q12 **D** Moving from left to right along each row, the corner shape moves one corner clockwise. Moving down each column, the dividing line that runs across each figure is consistent in placement and line type. In each column and row, the black dots appear once each in a group of one, two and three. Therefore, the answer is D.